52

Week

Success Plan

**LIFE CHANGING PRINCIPLES
FOR GREATER WEALTH,
HAPPINESS & HEALTH
THAT YOU CAN LEARN
- IN 5 MINUTES OR LESS -**

Dr. Bart Rademaker
#1 Best Selling Author, Speaker

52

#1
Best Seller

Week

Success Plan

LIFE CHANGING PRINCIPLES
FOR GREATER WEALTH,
HAPPINESS & HEALTH
THAT YOU CAN LEARN
- IN 5 MINUTES OR LESS -

52WeekSuccessPlanBook.com

ISBN: 978-0692607237

Printed in the United States of America

Printed by:

Abundant Press
Publish - Promote - Profit - Position - Platform
AbundantPress.com

Register This Book at:

52WeekSuccessPlanBook.com

For additional tips, resources, and videos

Medical Disclaimer

Although the author and publisher have made every effort to ensure that the information in this book was correct at press time, the author and publisher do not assume and hereby disclaim any liability to any party for any loss, damage, or disruption caused by errors or omissions, whether such errors or omissions result from negligence, accident, or any other cause.

The information provided in this book is designed to provide helpful information on the subjects discussed. This book is not meant to be used, nor should it be used, to diagnose or treat any medical condition. For diagnosis or treatment of any medical problem, consult your own physician. The publisher and author are not responsible for any specific health or allergy needs that may require medical supervision and are not liable for any damages or negative consequences from any treatment, action, application or preparation, to any person reading or following the information in this book. References are provided for informational purposes only and do not constitute endorsement of any websites or other sources. Readers should be aware that the websites listed in this book may change.

This book is designed to provide information and motivation to our readers. It is sold with the understanding that the publisher is not engaged to render any type of psychological, legal, or any other kind of professional advice. The content of each article is the sole expression and opinion of its author, and not necessarily that of the publisher. No warranties or guarantees are expressed or implied by the publisher's choice to include any of the content in this volume. Neither the publisher nor the individual author(s) shall be liable for any physical, psychological, emotional, financial, or commercial damages, including, but not limited to, special, incidental, consequential or other damages. Our views and rights are the same: You are responsible for your own choices, actions, and results.

This book is not intended as a substitute for the medical advice of physicians. The reader should regularly consult a physician in matters relating to his/her health and particularly with respect to any symptoms that may require diagnosis or medical attention.

Table of Contents

Introduction

Whatever you consistently focus on you become. Whatever you consistently do not focus on – you become as well. Each is the direct result of the quality of questions you habitually ask yourself each day. If you can ask yourself better questions, then you will get better answers. Sometimes the problem is simply we don't have the right question to ask ourselves.

This book is about asking those questions: new ones and better ones and to find new great solutions for our lives. Each question is designed to inspire you and become the stepping stone to making new and better decisions in your life and deliver the progress, the success and fulfillment you desire.

This book is also about offering you new solutions to the questions. These solutions are habits. As Anthony Robbins says: "show me your habits and I will show you your destiny". What you consistently do every day and what you consistently do in private or in public, is what you will be rewarded with. By asking the right question to determine what you really want will lead you to the right answers and habits.

You can read the entire book all at once and start a new habit each week. You can cherry pick throughout the book to whatever inspires your interest. You can work on any combination you desire – it all depends on your motivation for change.

We do recommend that each new habit is practiced diligently for an entire week – 7 days to determine if a new habit is one that you will like to continue. Give yourself the chance to fully experiment and experience a new habit because whatever new habit you choose, it will change the way you live your life. If you are a super achiever – then work on three new habits at once – not more. If you want to achieve even more than that – then dive into a personal growth program. Once you decide on a habit you like – keep doing it as it will serve you well.

Dedication

To my three amazing children: Brent, Evan and Gabriella

To all my past, present and future clients

To all my mentors over the years whose wisdom is now part of this book written for you. And for all those who want to make a change in their lives.

- 1 -

The Power Of Gratitude

What are you grateful for? What in your life do you take for granted? What could you be grateful for?

Gratitude is pleasing, it feels good and it's motivating. Gratitude is the celebration of the present and an acknowledgment that good things are in life. Gratitude is a conscious choice or a spontaneous one to affirm what is great in life. In gratitude you say "yes" to life and its gifts.

Gratitude has many benefits ranging from enhancement of happiness, joy, pleasure and overall health. Boosts the immune system, helps with pain and discomforts, reduces stress and blood pressure. Gratitude also promotes optimism, openness and forgiveness.

How often do you incorporate this state of gratitude actively in your life and can you recognize the benefits? What if you developed that habit to find much more gratitude in your life? What if the challenges, traumas and other toxic emotions in your life could be reversed?

Experiencing it daily increases levels of energy, optimism, empathy and motivation.

Every day for 5 or ten minutes, preferably in the morning, out loud, describe what you are grateful for or what you could be grateful for. When people start – they usually begin with thanking the people you know that recently did something for you. As time and experience goes, you will have all sorts of past memories that you thought you forgot and you thank those experiences, people or things that impacted you – even the negative ones.

Negative ones may have motivated you or saved you in one form or another. As you begin to run out of people to thank, then you start thanking what is around you until one day you realize that you are grateful for the air, the wind, the sun, and plain old existence.

Do this every day and you might find yourself doing it throughout the day. It will surprise you what you can be thankful for. There will be things you won't want to thank – just let those go – no one is forcing you to do that.

You can combine this exercise with working out or just a fast walk. But do it fully engaged in the process of gratitude – it is not effective if you are distracted by the TV or people around you.

Create a gratitude journal.

For more resources read or listen to material from the leading expert on gratitude Robert Emmons. In our resource section you will also find various book titles, audio titles as well as various internet links that can help you.

A commitment to this daily ritual will change the color of your life forever. Even the most successful people in the world realize that all their success is nothing without the state of gratitude.

REMEMBER

The vibration of gratitude attracts more abundance -Bart Rademaker

Resource: GRATITUDE

http://www.drrademaker.com/power-of-gratitude
Gratitude is the gateway to all that is possible
-Bart Rademaker

- 2 -

Don't Complain All Day

Did you complain about anything today? If something is not to your liking – are you likely to view this as a problem or an opportunity? Are you likely to feel that you have been wronged in some way or have you decided that stuff just happens? Is your mindset: "let's do something about it" or "let it go"?

Depending on your perspective: Complaining is a behavior that can either be disempowering or productive. Are you aware of your particular outcome when complaining? Is it simply to either bring awareness to a particular situation so that change can be brought about or simply a means to vent displeasure? Do you want a public acknowledgement or are you processing to let it go?

When complaining is disempowering – it is used to satisfy some of our behavioral needs like connection or significance. If I complain enough I can be significant and I can connect with others. Sometimes complaining is used to get the attention of others as a vehicle to satisfy their needs or to validate a victim state and making life not their fault.

By complaining – you focus on what you don't want and the universe will respond by giving it to you still. If complaining is not part of a productive process to empower you more then stop! In fact, why not just commit to no complaints whatsoever for one entire week: commit to not focusing on what you don't want and focus on what you do want.

As tempting or necessary as it may seem – commit to no complaints, only opportunities. Notice the moment that you are wanting to complain and stop immediately. Give it no energy whatsoever. Acknowledge that something is distasteful as if you were a third party, and leave the emotion out of it. Know that "life-challenges" and "life-pains" are inevitable but suffering is a choice we make.

Suffering is your mental or emotional response to the event or stimulus, and it is not necessary. So stop all complaints for an entire day and notice how you feel at the end of it.

Complaints carry a lot of negative energy with them: associations or triggers of other negative past experiences or potential future ones. There is anger in the words you say to yourself which then creates negative imbalances in your physiology. Furthermore, complaints close the door to spontaneous or natural positive alternatives. When the focus is on the negative, you are not focusing on what might be possible. The more negatives you have the more anchors you have to this state.

Each time there is a temptation to criticize – ask yourself rather – what do you really want? How does the complaint serve me? What would serve me better? Be curious and stop wanting and having a complaint in your thoughts. Just acknowledge that something is not to your liking and herein lies an opportunity for change.

There are several tricks that may help you: Do more stress relieving activities like meditation, yoga, gratitude, visualization. In a distasteful situation – change your perspective of the situation – ask yourself, what does this mean, what does this really mean, and what could be great about this situation?

Finally – take responsibility of your own contribution to the situation – what can you do to avoid it. This is particularly empowering and a learning experience for the future and for others – and your contribution.

<u>REMEMBER</u>
Dream more – Complain less -Bart Rademaker

Resource: Don't complain
http://www.drrademaker.com/dont-complain-all-day/

- 3 -

Motion and Stretch

Does any part of your day include a focused time to move or stretch your body?

60% of the American population does not move regularly and another 25% does not move at all! Our bodies are designed to move and when they don't – the body tightens, stiffens, degenerates and significantly increases the risk for debilitating disease and death. Our modern life fosters much less motivation to move due to long sedentary positions behind computers, desks, workstations and even factory lines so that work demands can be met.

Your body is your temple and the very foundation of your entire existence. To not take care of it – you limit yourself. The longer you ignore the need to properly take care of your body – the more the body will wear down and lose functionality over time that might be irreversible. Agile old people who can dance without pain do so because they have moved their entire lives and still dance in their 80's, 90's and 100's! There is no reason you can not do the same – in fact your very well being and ability to enjoy life is at stake if you don't.

Some very specific facts to mention:

Motion and stretching result in the following: increase joint lubrication, flexibility and range of motion, enhanced muscle elasticity, improved posture and decreased risk of injuries. Motion and stretch improves the circulation in the body and helps the removal of toxins from the body by the stimulation of the lymphatic channels in the body.

It helps with relaxation, stress relief, and produces increased levels of endorphins.

What to do – at the very minimum you must stretch and move the body every day. Passive stretch and stretch in motion are two different techniques. Some suggest that stretching with fluid motion is more beneficial and natural. Do not over stretch.

First just focus on the individual joints – make all sorts of repeated movement along the maximum range of motion for each joint. Start with the toes, then ankles, knees and so forth. Experiment with any motion but not to the extreme. Spend a minimum of ten minutes just activating all the joints you can find in your body and yes, you jaw is a joint to.

Start gently first thing in the morning as you get up or even in bed. Your outcome is to actually enjoy the process and imagine how the body benefits from the exercise: visualize how the joints get lubricated so that they are healthier, sense how blood circulates more through the body and imagine how the lymphatic drainage system is removing toxins from your tissues.

Additional tools include YouTube videos, stretch and motion cards, books on motion, stretching aids and rebounder.

REMEMBER
Life is motion -Bart Rademaker

Resource: Motion and Stretch
http://www.drrademaker.com/motion-and-stretch/

- 4 -

Daily Affirmations & Inspirations

An affirmation is a declaration of a truth whilst inspirations can move us emotionally to be creative or to a higher level of consciousness. Repeated declarations (affirmations) and   inspirations will affect the neural networks (of nerve cells) in the brain. This is called neuroplasticity and it is the brain's ability to adjust to repeated external and internal stimuli.

If we take advantage of this neuroplasticity - we can train ourselves and the function of our brain to move our lives in a direction that serves us better. The brain creates faster and or larger neural pathways that supports our actions and behaviors to make it easier to attain our goals.

By constantly focusing on what we really want and how we can get it – we will foster the creation of these neural pathways to live life on our terms.

In the context of this ritual – we define these declarations as simply the truths that you are already certain of. In order to develop new truths and habits, decide which truths or habits you want that improve your life or help you achieve the goals you want.

Regularly (multiple times per day) read or repeat to yourself affirmations or inspirational quotes that you completely connect with or desire to connect with even more deeply. An affirmation that you don't agree with may actually result in a counterproductive result and these must be avoided. Your commitment to the belief of the affirmation is critical. Each affirmation is meant to help develop the truths you can or already believe in or want to believe in.

Create a list of affirmations, read from a book or go online. Anthony Robbins uses the technique of incantations which is a very powerful tool to help you focus and your truths and your intention.

Here are some samples of affirmations:

- The best gift a man can give a woman is his time, his attention and his love
- The less you respond to negative people, the more peaceful your life will become
- It's a slow process, but quitting won't speed it up

Here are several incantations that Anthony Robbins uses:

- I believe, I do not doubt
- I create, I do not destroy
- I am a force for good not evil

Anthony Robbins is a master in helping people make the shifts they desire in life and uses incantations as part of the strategy for change. Sign up for an event or a life coach to experience this.

REMEMBER

You become what you constantly focus on, affirmations are our reminders
-Bart Rademaker

Resource: Daily affirmations and inspirations

http://www.drrademaker.com/daily-affirmations-and-inspirations/

- 5 -

Results / Outcome Focused Day

Are you fulfilled? Are your days productive, fulfilling and focused on getting results? Are they pretty much the same routine every day? Or are they full of unexpected events and reactionary to these events?

As you review your typical day, do you get up in the morning and set time aside to decide what your day will be like, what you will focus on, what your mindset will be or what you will achieve on that day?

Most people have lost the magic of living because they follow the same routine every day without giving themselves the opportunity to create new experiences and more fulfillment. Their daily routine is repeated each day without much variety, newness or specific intentions. This happens because they fail to have defined new fulfilling outcomes within their daily routine.

If you want to have more fulfillment each day – live each day with very specific intentions or outcomes. Create new meaningful outcomes with **all** the activities you do each day. Here are some examples of meaningful outcomes you can define right before the action:

For each meal:
Instead of satisfying the need to eat, plan on an energizing healthy and satisfying meal whilst creating a wonderful connection with the surrounding environment. Experience each bite with full awareness of taste, texture, smell and the thoughts they evoke.

Exercise: Instead of just working out, plan on an invigorating workout experience that helps build more strength, stamina, agility and coordination whilst removing the toxins out from the body and generating stress relief. Experiment with new exercises or routines and enjoy the process.

Phone calls: Instead of just calling a friend, plan on creating a deeper connection with friend or family whilst sharing new exciting experiences of the day and discover more reasons to be grateful for this connection and friendship.

House cleaning: Instead of cleaning up the mess, plan on creating a beautiful tranquil and clutter free home environment where the family feels charged up because this is a great home to live in.

Conversations: Instead speaking all the time, witness them, plan on having a great connection and discover what the other party is really saying or needing and focus on listening and being present.

Down time: Instead of watching TV, plan on taking care of your mind and spirit in ways that truly serve you the most and creates more fulfillment and gratitude in your life.

The purpose of this habit is to find a greater experience and more fulfillment each 24 hour period by focusing on the easy short term goals: the next phone call, the next meal, the next work out, the next conversation or the entire day. A vaguely or ambiguously stated outcome or intention gives a mediocre experience.

Ask the question: what can be greater about the upcoming activity or day that I would like to have? By deciding on a more meaningful and specific experience or outcome with clearly defined details – each activity and therefore the entire day can be more on purpose and fulfilling. If you prefer, you can also decide on an specific intention or mindset during the activity or the entire day.

REMEMBER

Focus on greater outcomes and receive greater rewards
- Bart Rademaker

Resource: Results / Outcome Focused Day
http://www.drrademaker.com/results-outcome-focused-day/

Register This Book at:

52WeekSuccessPlanBook.com

**For additional tips,
resources, and videos**

- 6 -

The Power Of Focusing
On One Thing

Are you a multi-tasker? Do you regard yourself super-efficient because you can multi task?

In this era of modern technology – many believe that multitasking is needed to be successful, and is often a recruiting requirement or a badge of honor. The truth is very different:

Research has proven that cognitive abilities are impaired, productivity drops by 20-40%, there is a decrease in the quality of the work performed, and there is increased stress and overwhelm. Brain studies show that we cannot focus on two different high level brain functions at the same time. What we actually do is shift very quickly between tasks. This shifting from one to another task is where we lose time and the ability to perform at the highest level. A Person engaged in this multi-tasking habit are more easily distracted and generally have weaker self-control (they cannot stay focused till the completion of the task).

The executive part of the brain uses its resources to manage one high level activity at a time. Whilst simple (automatic – unconscious) tasks can be handled simultaneously, complex ones can not. The brain can not decide between writing a particular word you are texting in one conversation and decide on a word with an entirely different conversation at the same time. Each of your thoughts is focused on one thing at time – two thoughts cannot occupy the same space in time. Actions require thinking and therefore can not be accomplished at the same time without rapid shifting. This rapid shifting is inefficient for the brain and results in higher levels of stress and less fulfillment and poorer results.

Multi tasking can even be dangerous: texting whilst driving accounts for 25% of all car accidents today. Five seconds to answer an incoming text is equivalent to driving blind over the length of a football field. Life and death situations arise in a split second, in fact, you are six times more likely to be in an accident whilst texting compared to driving under the influence.

Focus and flow results in a complete experience in that moment, a greater meaning and much more creativity, insight and fulfillment as well as the quality of the activity. More gets done in less time and it is done better and experienced better. This is also referred as mindfulness and being in the moment.

Ritual: Whatever it is that you are doing at any given time – commit to just that. Singularly commit to one task at a time - be it a conversation, reading, cooking dinner, social media, working etc. You will be rewarded on many levels. Notice and journal for yourself the difference. Is there less stress, are you more grounded, is the experience more full, are you aware of more things?

Commit to one entire week to singularly focus on one thing at a time. Every time you remember something or you feel the need to redirect your focus because you believe you will forget to do something that is important, either write a note on a pad for later referral or commit each day to effective planning and scheduling.

REMEMBER
FOCUS Spelled out means: Focus -- One – Course – Until – Successful.
Focus and enjoy a full experience.

Resource: The Power of Focusing on One Thing
http://www.drrademaker.com/the-power-of-focusing-on-one-thing/

- 7 -

Questions To Ask Yourself During The Day

What a man thinks - he becomes. The quality of our life is a direct result of the questions we habitually ask specific questions about ourselves.

Anthony Robbins has identified that we habitually ask ourselves a specific questions about ourselves, others, or life. The answer we give to these questions is the experience we ultimately have.

We typically have 70,000 thoughts each day of which 90% are the same thoughts of the day before and most of them are answers to our own questions. By being more selective and conscious to the questions we ask – our life experience can become much more full. The purpose of all these questions is to enhance your awareness as to how you live your life in the moment. With that higher awareness, you will have the opportunity to make smarter decisions.

1. What am I focusing on and what does it mean? In any given situation, there are many different things you can focus on. Different people watching the exact same event have a completely different experience because they all focused on very different parts of the event. When you are conscious of what you are focusing on, then decide: what it means. The meaning we give anything is the experience it becomes. With the meaning we often attach an emotion.

2. What am I doing about it? Our behavior at any given time is based on the decision we make as a result of the first two questions. Being more conscious of these questions results in more purposeful behavior and living.

3. What is my mood right now? What is your state right now? Angry, happy, sad, or excited? We experience life through the filters or the lens of our own emotion. The state or emotion may affect the meaning of any situation and thus your response to it.

4. What do I want.... What do I really want? We have our own rules as to why we choose what we want to do next: consciously or unconsciously. At any given moment we can make many different choices. Make it a habit to be honest with yourself in answering this question. The most successful people think about what they want in advance and are prepared when the time comes. They also ask the question: What will getting x,y,z do for me? And they know specifically what their outcome is and why they want it.

5. What stops me from getting what I want? If you are not moving forward with your outcome ask the question – what is stopping you? The simple awareness of not moving forward many be enough to move forward. Ask : what can I do to get what I want? Another question is to ask: what would you do if you could not fail? What new resource can you tap into to succeed?

6. What would happen if I didn't do this – What will it cost me now or in the future? If we are stopped – we are focusing on why we can't and forget to focus on what we don't get. Be clear – what happens when you don't move forward, what will you miss out on? Who else will lose? What will you gain?

7. What do I need to believe is true about myself ? Beliefs are our statements of our truths. It defines our identity and therefore most of how we live our lives. Find your truth or one you want to have. This can be generative in creating the success you desire because of what you believe about yourself.

<u>REMEMBER</u>

"The Quality of Life is the Quality of questions." -Anthony Robbins

Resource: Questions to ask yourself during the day

http://www.drrademaker.com/7-questions-to-ask-yourself-during-the-day/

Register This Book at:

52WeekSuccessPlanBook.com

**For additional tips,
resources, and videos**

- 8 -

Listen To Your Body

Do you notice any ache, pain or discomfort in your body? Do you crave certain foods? Do you always drink when you are thirsty?

Your body is your temple! Without your body – you would not be! Most people take this fact very much for granted. Do you? A Body in a poor state – results in life experiences that are poor! Keep it up, and you will endure much pain and suffering through life. By disregarding the body's signals or warnings now - will have serious implications in your future health history, vitality, energy and ability to do what you want.

Western culture is finally waking from its social hypnosis and realizes the need to take care of the body. Though-out time, most successful people have had very able bodies because they respected and listened to their body which enabled them to function at the highest level.

Not taking care of your body are at least not responding to its signals is a bad habit. There are many reasons for this, and they can be unlearned. Not taking care of the body is destructive to the body in the short term as well as the long term, and our body will alert us by responding with various signals like heartburn, headaches, joint pain or nervousness. However, social hypnosis tells us that these signals are a normal part of life and aging and all you need to do is take a pill!

Your body intelligence is sending out a smoke signal for you to stop now. You body is a beacon of information to your brain and your brain has an inner dashboard that registers the irregularities caused by the bad habit. Now it is time to respond to these signals with a higher awareness and the appropriate action. In addition, shifts in mood are a result of what you do to your body.

Start noticing the following: any discomfort or unease, tension, tightness, ache, itch, irritation, burn in any part of the body throughout the day. Start noticing the feet, then ankles, knees, hips and so forth. Focus you attention on each one. Is their fatigue? Is there an imbalance, what do you notice? Is there peace, stability, comfort, joy in these parts? Are you hungry, faint, thirsty, tired? Give your body what it needs!

If you have trouble noticing then try a yoga or a meditation pose. Stand with your feet firmly on the ground at level of your hips. Close your eyes, relax, breathe easy deep breaths. Hands open to the side allowing yourself to be open to any of the signals you can feel in your entire body.

Once you begin to notice parts of the body on a regular basis – you will start to notice how the body responds to your various habits – especially the foods that you eat, what you drink and how you move or don't move for that matter. With each sensation – decide what it really means. Indigestion after a fatty meal clearly suggest that your body disapproves. An ache in the knee because you have been sitting all day long suggests that you should move more. An approving ache in the muscles after a hard work lets you know that you got it right.

Commit to listening to your body all day long and make better decisions. In addition, shifts in mood are a result of what you do to your body.

REMEMBER
The body never lies – listen to it! -Bart Rademaker

Resource: Listen to Your Body
http://www.drrademaker.com/listen-to-your-body/

- 9 -

Commit To Finishing The Job

Do you start projects and not finish? Is it easy to get distracted, go astray, take too long or just leave things left undone, unfinished?

The truth is: there is no real purpose to start an activity or project and then not finish it. Leaving things undone only leaves mental clutter and can be a distraction to otherwise more fulfilling experiences.

Simple commit to finish the project when you first start it. Always have this be your mindset. The secret to starting and finishing is to have a clear outcome, a compelling reason and a commitment to complete the task. Additionally, there is a need to be both practical and realistic in your ability to complete the activity or you need to find someone who can.

Be honest: Are you being smart in your planning and are you giving yourself the right amount of time to complete the job or not? Are you allowing yourself to be distracted whilst you are performing the job by something that is supposedly more urgent? These are often reasons why we do not complete the job in addition to the loss of the motivation or reason to perform the job. Fully associate with the pleasing experience or the rewards with doing the job as you move closer to completing the job.

Remember the mental clutter of unfinished work is a distraction. The clutter occupies mental space, energy and prevents you from being fully present in the next task. Completing the tasks when they naturally should be done is part of the habit of focusing, being practical and being honest not only in your ability to complete the job timely but deciding that you want to start and want to finish the job!

The benefits of completion include:

- Higher sense of satisfaction
- Less stress because your mind is not trying to operate on many different levels (tasks) and needing to constantly make the decision – is it time to restart the task or not?
- Less stress because there is less clutter
- Higher quality of the work
- It impacts others and provides a higher sense of certainty for yourself and others
- You will manage your time better
- More productive
- And perhaps most important – you get to fully experience the results of a completed task!
- Boosts confidence and fulfillment
- Creates a habit!

REMEMBER

When things are done – creative space opens for more -Bart Rademaker

Along the philosophy of Tao: when less is done, less is left undone – so choose wisely what is to be done.

Resource: Commit to Finishing the Job

http://www.drrademaker.com/commit-to-finishing-the-job/

- 10 -

Target Your Time

What percentage of your time is spent doing what you really want to do and feeling great and in the zone whilst you are doing it? How much of your time is an experience of fulfillment and on purpose?

Tony Robbins has masterfully identified how we can divide our attention into 4 zones:

1. Zone of fulfillment (important but not urgent)
2. Zone of stress (important and urgent)
3. Zone of delusion (urgent but not important)
4. Zone of distraction (not important and not urgent)

Remaining in that zone of fulfillment more than 60% of the time is the ideal. In this zone you are planning and scheduling effectively and get to enjoy life more fully without too much stress or non-productivity.
Where do you spend most of your time?

For an entire week – commit to honestly rating yourself during the day time for each of these categories. If you realize that you are spending less than 60% of your time in the zone of fulfillment – ask yourself – what can you do to increase this time?

Health benefits will be clear:
- More satisfaction
- Better self-esteem
- Feeling whole and complete
- Feeling happier
- More time to connect and be on purpose in life.

Determine what is really important each day, what does each activity really contribute to your well being? Are activities like watching tv, (news, soap operas), Facebook, etc. really contributing to your higher self and purpose? Do they help you with feeling better about life and yourself? Am you growing or doing something to improve your life or that of another? Are you taking care of yourself like you should? Are you avoiding something you really should be doing now?

There can be a tendency to avoid the important whilst it is still not urgent because we are not clear what needs to be done or because we are tired or because doing it causes more pain than pleasure. Hiding in the zone of distraction or delusion will not help matters - now or in the future, in fact they will typically lead to the zone of stress. Find a strategy to engage in the important and not urgent before it gets into the zone of stress. Tony Robbins has a great resource called RPM – a simple system of thinking that creates an extraordinary life.

A more simplified approach is to block schedule your day in five categories or less to include at least the following:

1. Sleep
2. Work/Mission/School
3. Personal / Private time

These three categories are absolute "musts" and it is important to allocate the right amount of time for each. Most people need eight hours of sleep, will want to work eight hours per day and give yourself at least two hours per day for personal / private time (exercise, meditation, personal growth, etc). That leaves six hours for everything else – including your decision for the non urgent and not important time. By following and committing to a simple block schedule like this – you can target your time more effectively because it is easier to commit to a simple system. You can find more balance and harmony as well as fulfillment.

REMEMBER
Target your time – live a life full of meaning -Bart Rademaker

Resource: Target your time
http://www.drrademaker.com/target-your-time/

Register This Book at:

52WeekSuccessPlanBook.com

**For additional tips,
resources, and videos**

- 11 -

Ask For What You Want And Be Prepared To Get It!

Are you living life on your terms? Is life happening to you or for you? Living in a dream is different than living the dream. How often do you connect with your true purpose or mission in life? Do you have one? How often are you actively and consciously aware of what you want in life? Or is life too busy for you and you gave up on your dreams?

Success leaves clues, and the most successful people have a clear vision and mission in life and a reason for it! They seem to live life with passion! They seem to live life on their terms and have everything they want. The difference that creates the difference – they made two decisions.

1. They know what they want and why – and they asked for it!
2. They made a commitment to get it – and they were prepared to get it!

Discover what your true passion is or re- energize an old one. If there were no limitations of money, education or experience and you could not fail – what would you do or be?

The first step must involve writing it down. Find a time where you will not be interrupted, where you can get inspired and creative and visualize what you really want in life! Answer these questions: What do you really want? Why do you want this? Why will it be so great to have it? How do you benefit from this? Who do you become when you have it? How will others benefit from this? What will you feel when you achieve it? What is now possible that was not before? Who will you meet? Who are your friends or partners? What do you have in life? When do you want to achieve it? How will you know you have it? What would it cost you if you didn't have it that you will not tolerate anymore?

27

Now re-write it on 3 by 5 cards, and use short inspiring statements that are easy to read, and that excite you! Make sure you have easy access to these cards at all times and frequently refer to them and feel the excitement as if you already have it. Actively visualize / experience it as if it is already happening. Create a picture of it and notice what you see, hear and feel and what you say to yourself in this moment of achieving your goal. Write this down. On each card you must also write down what you are committing to do to achieve the outcome. Now fully associate the entire experience that you visualized earlier as if it happened with any activity you are committing to that will bring you to your final goal.

On a separate card - what are the things you really don't want in your life – watching TV, reading the newspaper, organizing and reorganizing the same thing or what are the things you don't stand for any more. This card you only read once a day.

By constantly being attentive to what you want, visualizing it, feeling it, believing it, you become more aligned with the possibilities for creating exactly what you want. By constantly stating what you want, be prepared to receive it!

REMEMBER
Dare to dream and dream big. Whatever the mind can think of – it can conceive.

Resource: Ask for what you want and be prepared to get it!
http://www.drrademaker.com/ask-for-what-you-want-and-be-prepared-to-get-it/

- 12 -

Being Present

Do you practice being present or being in the moment – also known as mindfulness?

"The secret of health for both mind and body is not to mourn for the past, not to worry about the future, or not to anticipate troubles, but to live in the present moment wisely and earnestly." ~Buddha

The art of mindfulness is about focusing on what is happening right now. Experiencing life in all of its elements as they present themselves to you in this very moment and not allowing yourself to be distracted by either internal thoughts or external events.

Each moment is potentially a magnificent gift in all the manners that we can experience them. As each moment passes – that opportunity is now lost unless it was taken in that moment. To singularly focus on a situation is to benefit from everything that moment has to offer. To miss a single item of that situation may change the meaning or experience entirely. It is no different than watching a movie – if your eyes turn away – you may miss a vital clue to the story.

Mindfulness enhances meaning and fulfillment. Enhances understanding and appreciation. Enhances opportunities for self and others. It can bring more peace, clarity and joy to your life.

The practice is simple – focus on what is immediately in front of you. Notice everything there is to notice in regards to the situation at hand. Notice how you feel, think and respond to it.

Choose to surrender to the moment and receive the full gift of the moment rather than thinking or anticipating what is next.

This is especially true in conversations. If you notice that your thoughts wander off – gently come back to the moment – reengaging on what is immediate in front of you. Being in the moment is a habit that requires practice.

Ways to be present: By noticing that you are focused on the moment. You can also ask yourself if you are present. To help stay in the moment – feel the ground at your feet and feel yourself breathing as you connect with self and your surroundings – dispelling any distractions. Practice this often – even if it is for a moment. If you are talking to someone, put away your cell phone, if you are sitting with your family at the dinner table – focus and hear what others are saying and wait to give your response. When you are chewing your food – notice the different tastes and textures.

If being present was an important practice 25 centuries ago – it certainly must be in our busy world today!

REMEMBER
Being present is a gift for you and it is that gift for another
-Bart Rademaker

Resource: Being present
http://www.drrademaker.com/being-present/

- 13 -

Focus On What Is Great
– The Art Of Reframing –

Are you naturally wired to see what is wrong before you see what is right? Are you more likely to pay attention to the news when the story is about a looming disaster or a charity event?

Our reptilian brain is engineered to respond to the physical dangers around us – so naturally our higher brain centers will also be hyper critical of the surrounding environment. Unless you are wired to always be positive, you may have the tendency to observe what is wrong about something before you see what is right. Our ability to be objective about surrounding dangers can indeed be very helpful until it is not.

The purpose of reframing is an opportunity to create a more positive or constructive meaning and or experience in any given situation and enhance the quality of life. The art of reframing starts with the habit of asking this question: is this a threat or an opportunity? Is this positive or negative?

In order to fully transmute an experience into a more positive one, several steps need to happen.

1.   Decide what the meaning is of the situation
2.   Find what is great about the situation
3.   Decide what can be better about the situation

In any given situation ask yourself – in one year's time (or more) how would you have liked to have shown up in that situation – did you create the best meaning, experience and learning?

There is always a benefit to appreciate in the moment, a better meaning, or any learning that help you grow or be happier.

Our emotional response may hinder your ability or desire to reframe the situation. In this event acknowledge the presence of the negative emotion, imagine yourself looking upon that person that is you with the experience and the emotion and ask yourself as the impartial onlooker to that person the three questions above. Done correctly by dissociating from the event in this way you will be able to discover new meanings about the event that may support you at a higher level. Remember, past negative experiences serve as additional anchors to a negative belief. Be impartial to the past and the present and decide on a new better meaning.

The meaning you give something is the response you give it. Create a better meaning – create a better quality of life.

Whatever you focus on and indeed whatever you don't focus on becomes your destiny.

REMEMBER
Greatness lies in the moment that you choose it -Bart Rademaker

Resource: Focus on what is great – the art of reframing
http://www.drrademaker.com/focus-on-what-is-great/

- 14 -

The Law Of Requisite Variety
He Who Is Most Flexible
– Wins –

Are you ever rigid in your ways or thinking and discover that you have been bettered or left behind? There are countless of examples of major corporations that no longer exist because they refused to change with the times. How in your life does this happen – even at a smaller level? Do you stay in your comfort zone only to watch others have more fun or success because they did something different than you?

Being flexible means 'have more choices'. Happier people seem to have more choices. Having more choices – is also a choice. A choice to see things differently (reframing). A choice to have a certain outcome no matter what motivates one to find new choices when they don't appear right away. A choice to try again after you failed but try something new. A choice to feel uncomfortable, to take a risk and get out of the comfort zone. As Tony Robbins says: life begins outside of your comfort zone.

Choices are also beliefs and beliefs are statements of your own truth or what you know in your mind to be true. Having the belief that beliefs can be changed is also being flexible. Flexibility is also the nature of evolution. When environment changes and species adapt – they survive whilst those that don't change – die. Truth is – the only constant in life is change.

Having one option is no choice. Have two options is a dilemma. Have three options – now you have choices. (Tony Robbins)

Choices are also the path to experimentation – trying something new and different and see if it works. The biggest failure in life is failing to try.

33

Try means a new choice that may lead to exactly what you want. There is a saying in old Dutch "you already have a 'no' but you could get a 'yes'". "Yes to life" to results to new experiences by simply creating new choices.

Besides exercising on different choices, flexibility also means having the ability to sees things differently. Finding different meanings with each scenario leads to different opportunities or choices. Flexible means – being able to ask questions like – can this meaning something else? Is this really true? What do I not see? What do I not know?

Being flexible allows you to find a more natural or organic flow in your daily life with fewer upset than if you were more rigid and inflexible. Flexible does not mean settling – it means appreciating something differently.

REMEMBER:
In any given system – that element that is more flexible - wins.

Resource: The law of Requisite Variety
http://www.drrademaker.com/law-of-requisite-variety/

- 15 -

Stand Guard At
The Door Of Your Brain

Who do you listen to or get advice from? Are people supporting you or changing your ideas? Who or what influences you? Who is driving your bus, you or someone else's influence?

"Who is driving the bus?" is a great quote and book title of <u>Bandler and Grinder</u>. It relates to which voices are dictating what you believe, value and do. These voices are simply programs that you have taken on for yourself from other people (parents, siblings, mentors and others). These programs (known as memes), are patterns of thinking and behaving that can be largely unconscious and to determine what you do or achieve in life.

Any voice around us has the potential to change us. Any voice can influence us to even violate our deepest values and beliefs if there is enough leverage. It is therefore important to at all times, stand guard at the door of your brain. Have a process in place to understand how others can influence you and cause you to think or behave differently than what may be best for you. Also have a process by which you feed your mind with the ideas of great thought leaders.

STAND GUARD TO THE DOOR OF YOUR BRAIN

Notice how words affect you: positive or negative.

- Do the words inspire you and serve you?
- Do they cause you to take action – and what effect does it have on you?
- When words do not support you or violates what you believe in or value, notice what you do?

- Is your response serving you or hindering you?
- Who can you consistently listen to that will give you supportive or inspirational ideas?
- Who can help you grow?
- Why do you consistently listen to words that will not support all of mankind?
- Do the words support a greater good?

REMEMBER:

What you feed your mind is what you become! So Get Smart! Words can be good for you, good for others and good for the great good. -Bart Rademaker

Resource: Stand Guard at the Door of your Brain.

http://www.drrademaker.com/stand-guard-at-the-door-of-your-brain/

- 16 -

Letting The Inner Child Out

Animals play, children play, do you? When was the last time you had untethered fun?

What would it be like if your inner child came out to play every day? What if you could re-ignite that sense of adventure, abandon, optimism, grandeur, spontaneity, invention or whatever you remember it was like as a child? And if you can't remember, what would it be like if your child could come to play and find the joy and excitement to unapologetically embrace all of who we are (faults and all) and simply play with abandon?

What would it be like for you to have these experiences on a regular basis? How much more fun would it be in this life that wants to be so serious all the time? Stress is a burden, playful joy is healing. Get some healing in your life at least once a week OR BETTER YET - EVERYDAY!

What adult games can you play that mimicked the ones you once played as a child? What games can you play with kids that re-ignite childhood experiences? What games did you play as a child or always wanted to play but could not? Or how can you simply be playful with your family, friends, colleagues and even pets? Watch the stuff that makes the kids laugh. Life is grand in a child's view, full of imagination – let it flow as you walk in nature – play hide and seek in the woods and win for once! Let the competitive child come up and win when as a child you could not.

What were some of the fond memories of trips or excursions that you had? Do them again. Be bratty, do a practical joke, be sneaky. Put fun music on and dance like crazy, splash in puddles after the rain, wave at people you don't know and smile.

This is not a time to censor your actions and be concerned about outside opinions. What are you passionate about – what puts a smile on your face?

Did you have Lego, Barbie dolls, toy cars, models, maybe it's time to bring them out again. Do a pillow fight or make a fort out of sheets, boxes or your favorite construction material. Chase butterflies, make papier Mache masks, draw pictures, paint, and if you did not do any of these as a child – do them now with your inner child and laugh and be messy and mess it up knowing that it's ok. Find your favorite candy, ice cream or food as a child and reminisce those time now. Play an organized sport for just the joy of playing and competing and winning and losing.

Inside of every older person is a younger person - Lighten up be playful connect with the inner child. Our brains are wired to seek – this then releases dopamine in the system which makes us feel good. Playing is a form of seeking.

Playing is essential for all ages. Benefits of play time: Source of relaxation, improved mood and wellbeing, stimulate and challenges the brain in a positive manner. Induces competitive spirit as well as a cooperative one. Improves imagination, creativity and problem solving abilities. Experience of joy, happiness, flexibility and a sense of freedom. Improves social skills, connection with others and helps relationships both casual and intimate ones with excitement, freshness, vibrancy and intimacy. Improves productivity, source of renewed energy and drive. Helps with recovery from stress. Improved energy, vitality, immune system, ability to fight of infections, ability to manage stress, cardiovascular improvement, mental agility, etc.

REMEMBER

How we play games is how we play life!

Resource: Letting the Inner child out!

http://www.drrademaker.com/letting-the-inner-child-out/

- 17 -

Time Out

Do you know what cerebral congestion is? Do you ever have moments where you just need to take a break from all the mental activity and noise? Do children really need a "time out" because of behavioral issues or could they possibly just need some downtime?

Why do we give children a time out when they misbehave? What most people don't realize is that their brain is actually in overload/overwhelm with too much information to process and they don't know how to behave and simply need the time to settle down.

Are you over done with modern life? Are you trying to handle multiple assignments / projects at the same time? Does it really feel good to do this? Being busy is not the same as being effective. Herein lies the problem: not being effective can be unfulfilling and even frustrating. This in turn can cause you to be overwhelmed, restless, anxious or simply unglued if not remedied in one form or another.

Typically, adults handle overwhelm much better than children, however it still can affect us negatively. More than that, we need time to think, to process, to relax, to dream and to be able to do this without all the extraneous busyness or noise that interrupts a natural progression in thought that the brain needs. This is a time to solve, resolve, let go and to recharge. Too much clutter or conflict in the brain takes up energy and can cause fatigue, and other issues.

Plan and schedule downtime. This is an important daily ritual. This can be a simple 3-5 minute practice of silence throughout the day. Sit or stand for this time, focus on breathing or "nothing" and when thoughts interrupt, notice this and let the thoughts go. (One way to focus on "nothing" is to ask the question – what is my next thought? – and notice the space of silence it creates). Another practice can also be a brief nap during the day (Some suggest 20 minutes between 1 and 4 pm). Or take a stroll outside without any purpose except to get away. There are many other ways to relax the brain and the purpose is to notice this happening.

This downtime can also be the practice of gentle reflection, of saying thanks before a meal. It also can be a moment of intention just before starting a project or activity. A way of being mindful and in alignment for the next time period of activity. An example could be one that Mark Divine (Unbeatable Mind) suggests before any workout routine: for 5 minutes reflect on the intention and outcome of the routine. You can do this before a meeting, a phone call or even a study period. This moment of downtime, of silence can create more satisfaction, fulfillment, purpose in daily activities by quieting the mind of distractions.

Of course the practice of meditation is a great way to find this downtime.

REMEMBER
Have downtime to enhance your uptime! -Bart Rademaker

Resource: Time out!
http://www.drrademaker.com/time-out/

- 18 -

Reframing

Do you ever have negative speak (disempowering or negative statements about yourself, your environment or other things)? Does it stop you in any way?

There may be times that we get stuck with a certain negative belief, idea or perspective that we believe is true and one which can stop us from achieving our desired outcomes. These negative beliefs can limit our experience of life in general and destroy our dreams. As Henry Ford put it: "Whether you think you can, or if you think you can't - you are right!"

Each time such a negative belief shows up – let it trigger two questions:

- Is this really true?
- What do I really want right now?

To help you eradicate this type of thinking - there is a simple exercise that you can do any time during the day.

Paper and pen: Draw a line down the middle of the page
Write down up to 5 negative beliefs about yourself in the left column (using 10 words or less).

In the right column – write the empowering opposite truth that you are or want to be. Keep it simple.

Examples:

I am bad	I am good, and I am great
I am lost	I know my way
I am confused	I am certain
I am not good enough	I am good enough
I am stupid	I am smart
I can't do this	I can do this

Any positive statement can be made even more colorful with even more meaningful words.

Example: Everything I do is for the greater good! I always find my way on the right time! I am certain in all my creative ways! I am all that I am and I am amazing! I am a genius in all that I do!

As you make these statements as you are or want to be, tell yourself why this is true. Give yourself reasons why this could be true or why you would want them to be true and as you can – feel the sensation of this truth in your body – notice the sensations in your body.

REMEMBER
We are what we choose to believe... we are! - Bart Rademaker

Resource: Reframing
http://www.drrademaker.com/reframing/

- 19 -

Personal Growth / Development

Have you noticed a sense of personal accomplishment, fulfillment or happiness when you are growing in useful knowledge or skills that open up new opportunities as well? Compared to your child or teenager years, how much less do you learn and grow consistently today? Do you know what personal development looks like and how much time do you actually dedicate daily or weekly to your own personal development?

Definition of personal growth (development) from Wikipedia:
"Personal development includes activities that improve awareness and identity, develop talents and potential, build human capital and facilitate employability, enhance quality of life and contribute to the realization of dreams and aspirations.

The concept is not limited to self help but includes formal and informal activities for developing others in roles such as teacher, guide, counselor, manager, life coach or mentor. When personal development takes place in the context of institutions, it refers to the methods, programs, tools, techniques, and assessment systems that support human development at the individual level in organizations."

Some keys facts to understand about growth in general:
- If a system is not constantly growing, it is dying
- If a system is not being used – it will stop working
- If you stopped at a green light – the world will pass you by

There are many ways to keep on growing that are best suited for you. Our minds and bodies are functioning the best when we are challenged to expand and grow. Bones, muscles, tendons get stronger when they are exercised and stimulated. New connections in the brain are constantly being created as the result of stimuli. It seems we are the happiest in growth and progress. In fact, there is a center of the brain, called the seeking center, that never becomes satiated by the stimuli it receives – in other words, it constantly needs to be stimulated.

Personal growth is therefore essential in life to be able to thrive in this ever changing world. As the phrase goes: "adapt or die" and this requires growth to adjust to the changes in the environment because the one constant in life is "change".

Personal development can be exciting as you acquire new insights, tools, skills that increase your opportunities and success in life. To not acquire these is akin to saying – "I will be at the effect of the world around me" or "I am not master of my own destiny".

When you understand and embrace the fact that each person is simply the summation of all their experiences, decisions and feelings, you understand that you are responsible for where you are today. There are no mistakes – only an unwillingness to learn, grow and transform unfavorable situations – however painful and unfair they may seem. To transform requires dedicated effort to grow beyond. The benefits are available to anyone.

The ritual: actively pursue some type of personal growth or development daily for 30 minutes. Over time this results in massive growth and the opening of new opportunities. See the resource page for ideas.

REMEMBER
The best of me is yet to come.. and the more ways I can grow – the more I become! -Bart Rademaker

Resource: Personal Growth / Development
http://www.drrademaker.com/personal-growth/

- 20 -

Routine Your Decisions

How much time do you really take to decide on what to do during the day? If your daily routine constantly changes, how does this affect your natural flow and well being?

Wasted time: Every day / week we have specific actions that we repeat over and over again. Studies have shown that if you do not schedule this time in advance, you waste significant times during each day making the decision to do one thing or another. You weigh the options, the benefits and downsides over and over again every day – this takes up valuable time.

Mental clutter: constantly outweighing the same different available options causes a mental clutter that distracts the brain from focusing on other important things in life. Less clutter helps clear the mind and produces more generative thinking.

Rhythm irregularities: as personal and professional lives can be very demanding as well as unpredictable, a structured approach to these daily challenges will make things easier. The body and mind function better if we follow daily / weekly rhythms. This is particularly evident with sleeping, eating, and movement rhythms throughout the day.

Establishing routines in advance, making the decisions only once rather than multiple times during the day or week – allows you to have less clutter, less wasted time, a better daily or weekly rhythm, more consistency with activities that can be nurturing and support to personal health and finally a more fulfilling experience since there is better focus and completion of tasks.

Remember – do you really need to be making the same decisions every day over and over again when once a day or once a week can be enough?

There are many time management systems and not the purpose of this book. RPM by Tony Robbins is by far one of the best simple systems to have an extraordinary life.

REMEMBER
Routine the routine so that extraordinary can be extraordinary! - *Bart Rademaker*

Resource: Routine your decisions.
http://www.drrademaker.com/routine-your-decisions/

- 21 -

How We Communicate Does Not Work

What is the word "listening" to you?

Can you hear and fully appreciate what someone is communicating to you and simultaneously thinking and formulating your response to them? It is tempting to think you can but the brain actually can't. What information do you lose, what subtle message do you miss when you don't give someone their full attention. It could be the difference between success and failure, an average relationship or an amazing one.

So what is listening? It is strictly the ability to accurately receive all the information that another is wanting to communicate. This includes all the information that is said as well all the information that is left unsaid. Listening is not about your filter, your projection or your response to the communication; that comes after the listening process is complete. The purpose to listening is to fully know what the other person wants or needs you to know – and then hear, (understand), what they say – without any judgment or any filtering!

Benefits of effective listening: Accurate Information and greater clarity. Increase likeability and respect. Better relationships, better experiences. Better results and less mistakes.

How listen: It begins with intention – have the intention to be present with the person in front of you and be curious without judgment. Be open. Maintain eye contact, and use the technique of rapport to match them.

Fade out any of the distractions around you and listen with all senses: notice words, tone, body language.

Listen to meaning, to feelings and listen to what is unsaid. Understand the very specific meaning of words rather than generalizing the meanings or making assumptions.

Acknowledge any thought or emotion that comes up in you - to yourself, and save them for later. "Take a deep breathe" or ground yourself by noticing your feet on the ground if you feel the need to respond right away or have an emotion you feel you can not contain (excitement, anger, whatever).

Acknowledge the speaker in what they are saying either verbally or nonverbally and help encourage the speaker to explore their thoughts so that they can convey their message more effectively by being patient.

Identify key messages and at the completion of their communique and question, clarify, paraphrase or offer what you understood what their communication was without adding your personal bias, prejudice or commentary. Stop being critical - this leads to assumptions that might be wrong and distort the true message.

If you are preparing to speak, you are not listening! Give the speaker time to explore their thoughts, be ok with pauses or silence – let them signal when they are done. Listening is an active process and a fundamental interpersonal skill.

REMEMBER
You have two ears and one mouth: The world is giving you answers every day – learn to listen! - Bart Rademaker

Resource: How we communicate does not work!
http://www.drrademaker.com/how-we-communicate-does-not-work/

- 22 -

The Art Of Compliments

What do you prefer – a compliment or a criticism? Which one do *you* give more of?

People like people like themselves. What we like in others is what we like in ourselves. The power of a compliment is that it increases the vibration of positivity. It makes people feel good about themselves when they receive genuine compliments. The person giving the compliment will also feel the positive effect.

Compliments:
- Show that you notice and are noticed
- Are the currency in motivation and actually enhances productivity in the workplace
- Enhances relationships and increases a positive flow in social settings
- Increases self esteem and well being in both the giver and receiver
- Promotes trust and reciprocity

"Compliments" is the currency in social settings - improving the overall experience. To be a real compliment these are some requirements:
- It must be genuine
- It must be unique
- It must be descriptive and with emotional context
- It must be concise
- It must not be qualified
- It must be appropriate for the time. Place, setting and context
- It must not have an agenda or expected return

As you can be generous with compliments you can find what is good and great in others even if there are parts that you disagree with. Identifying the good in others identifies the good in yourself.

49

The acknowledgment is powerful both for the giver and the receiver. Make an effort to find greatness in others and offer it freely. Step up this practice and find many rewards – do it daily at least 3 times.

REMEMBER
One kind word can change someone's entire day. (web)

Resource: The Art Of Compliments
http://www.drrademaker.com/art-of-compliments/

- 23 -

Selfish VS Self Actualized And Self Love

How much time do you dedicate to yourself? Are you ever first or first enough? Can you give yourself two to four hours each day for yourself and make it non negotiable?

Studies show that many people feel guilty when they take care of themselves. Out of guilt, which is mostly unconscious, we feel compelled to take care of others first because if we do not, we might get rejected or admonished.

The questions you will want to consider:
- Is it selfish to fulfill your own true potential? (Fulfilling true potential is known as self actualization)
- Is it selfish to give yourself self love? (Self love makes sure that you take care of yourself)
- Living your true potential and giving yourself self love is your own responsibility. In fact success in this area allows you to gift more of yourself in return to the world around you.

To become self actualized:
Be responsible to self. Realize what you truly want in life and for self. What does a snapshot of a day out of your life look like? How healthy or well are you? What have you given up that gives you happiness and fulfillment because of external demands? Are you actualizing your personal growth and ambition to improve your life? Are you fulfilled in all areas of life that matter for you?

Make sure that your personal, emotional, and physical needs are taken care of. Take the time to meditate, to think, to dream or just to shut down. Downtime is good for your wellbeing as well as creativity.

51

Realizing that others can be responsible for themselves allows you to take time for yourself.

Purposefully schedule time for self each and every day. Do what you like to do the most. Remember – it must include both a physical and mental break.

There are twenty four hours each day. Decide how many hours of sleep you really need (no cheating) – make this non negotiable. Now define how many hours you must work (this is negotiable). With the remaining hours left – define how many hours must be assigned to just you (non negotiable). This includes time to think, to dream, to create, to regenerate, to heal and to grow. These activities include meditation, exercise, creative time, personal growth or anything else that is strictly designed for self even though it may be accompanied by others like doing yoga or going for walks.

Remember: Self sacrifice is not fulfilling your purpose in life. Down playing our greatness does not serve anyone – including those that want you to downplay it! Finally – anyone who tells you not to follow your dreams is selfish – they want to keep you under their thumb!

The best catalyst for self actualization is a commitment to personal growth. Personal growth is multidimensional and an easy way to achieve it is by learning from those who have already mastered and have achieved their success. In your pursuit for personal growth, be in a state of high energy, curiosity, openness with a willingness to try new things and get out of your comfort zone – this is where real growth and change happens.

<u>REMEMBER</u>

Self actualize yourself and grow into the shoes that actually fit you- Bart Rademaker

Resource: 23 Selfish vs Self Actualized and Self Love

http://www.drrademaker.com/selfish-vs-self-actualized-and-self-love/

Register This Book at:

52WeekSuccessPlanBook.com

**For additional tips,
resources, and videos**

- 24 -

Journaling

How different would your life be today if you had complete and instant access to all the insights, learnings and wisdom you collected over your entire life? What if you could immediately recall all the great ideas, inventions or plans you have had? That's for starters! What if you journaled your entire life – and you could have been 20 or 40 years ahead of yourself right now – would you start now?

With 70,000 thoughts per day, surely you have had many great ideas, insights, plans, dreams, inventions and experiences! How many have you forgotten? Out of the billion or more thoughts, how many could be relevant today? It would be priceless if all this was somehow captured and documented for you.

In addition to simply recording and being able to recall any important event in life, the process of journaling has been proven to be healthy as well. Studies confirm the following:

Journaling helps with stress management by more effectively processing and releasing deep emotions, conflicts, challenges and finding solutions.

Journaling positively impacts blood pressure, lung function, immune system and other bodily systems.

Journaling helps you to explore and clarify your thoughts more deeply and holds the opportunity to be even more creative in the process.
Journaling enhances self esteem by reducing stress, processing challenges and capturing the great moments and celebrations.

Journaling is an active process helping the brain to more effectively process and remember through neuroplasticity and develop stronger neural networks in the brain where it matters.

The process of developing new neural networks can help you become even more creative by helping you stay focused and helps solve problems and develop new innovative ideas.

Journaling allows the brain to process a multitude of concepts more effectively – no different than a computer using a hard drive to read and write for faster computing whilst not using up all the ram.

Journaling records this information for later benefits like self knowledge, joy, living more on purpose and fulfilling life dreams. It permanently captures important moments, experiences, thoughts, feelings, problems, dreams or celebrations.

Journaling organizes thoughts for later retrieval and helps plan and capture goals and track progress and keeps you more accountable to yourself.

Journaling is best done handwritten since it activates more parts of the brain, integrates the process more deeply, helps with memory and cognitive function and the results are overall much better than the typed format. Typed can be more efficient in the form of saving and filing however a digital pen may be your answer.

Just think of the benefits of all your insights and ideas how they can help you and others and allow you to live your life on your terms.

REMEMBER
A life worth living is worth recording -Anthony Robbins

Resources: 24 Journaling
http://www.drrademaker.com/journaling/

- 25 -

Value Chain And Hierarchy

What do you value? What is important to you? And more importantly, what do you value consistently and in what order do they show up?

Think: what you value more determines what you do. For example, you value security much more than fun, you may be that person that will not jump out of an airplane with a parachute.

Values are intrinsic experiences that are desirable. They can be internally motivated or a result of an external experience. For example, many people value money (external) which gives them security (internal). Your awareness of what is really important to you will also affect what you do and do not do. Whenever there is a conflict between two opposing values, decision making may be confusing if not frustrating, unfulfilling to some degree and even impossible! Understanding what values you typically focus on will be very helpful in creating better balance and flow in your life. Write down both your internal and external values (examples below) in the order of importance. List up to 10 for each and then determine if there are any conflicts. Change the order as necessary.

Commit to being daily review of at least 3 values and have the intention to focus on these throughout the day and commit to specific decisions or actions throughout the day. By doing this you will set the tone and pace of your day with intention and positive results. It will help you to stay on the course you have decided is important to you even with the many distractions that may occur daily. Discover greater fulfillment and results.

Here is a partial list of examples of values you may want to consider. Check the resources for a more complete list as well as an explanation of means and ends values.

Gratitude	Happiness	Harmony	Health
Joy	Love	Passion	Security
Self Confidence	Success	Vitality	Wealth
Wisdom	Fun	Playfulness	Excitement

REMEMBER
What you truly value the most, you receive the most - Bart Rademaker

Resource: Value Chain And Hierarchy
http://www.drrademaker.com/value-chain/

- 26 -

Power Nap

Are you a workaholic and forgo getting enough sleep? Is it hard to get up in the morning or hard to concentrate in the afternoon? How about the afternoon energy dip, where you are less creative or productive – is any of this even slightly you? Do you ever take a nap during your working day?

Over 1/3 of the American population does not get enough sleep. Lack of sleep seriously inhibits performance on all levels. Research clearly shows that a power nap 20-30 minutes between 1 and 4 significantly improves performance and health! If major companies like google are instituting this in their business model, maybe they are on to something and it is time you incorporated this in your daily schedule.

Most people will struggle against their sleepiness throughout the day with or without aids like coffee or other energy drinks and supplements and try to function normally. However, this normally is unsuccessful, and it does not take care of the root problem that your body and mind must rest as the brain needs the time to process. Additionally, studies clearly prove reduced productivity, creativity, an increase in mistakes as well as other deficits.

While a power nap seriously helps cognitive performance and your health, drinking coffee actually reduces memory function, and not taking the nap reduces performance significantly.

There are different strategies to get an effective nap, however the easiest thing to do is plan it for daily consumption. For best results: Schedule it at a regular time during the day between 1 and 4.

Additionally, close the door, prevent interruptions, get comfortable, a dark room at a comfortable temperature is best. Use an eye mask or blanket if this helps you.

Each nap should be timed depending on what you are wishing to achieve. 20 – 30 minutes will revitalize you, improve your alertness. A 40-60 minute nap will help with cognitive memory processing and typically will also result in sleep inertia afterwards. A ninety minute nap will better support cognitive memory processing and usually does not cause any sleep inertia.

A set time can be accomplished either with an alarm or timed sound induction and waking program.

REMEMBER
Take a nap and change your life - Bart Rademaker

Resource: 26 Power Nap
http://www.drrademaker.com/power-nap

- 27 -

Enough Sleep

Most people need an average of 8 hours of sleep each day. The question is – how good is your sleep really? Are you having a hard time waking in the morning and have periods of sleepiness during the day or do you wake up easily each time without any mental slowdown during the day?

Our bodies do require a specific sleep and awake rhythm. Sleep is an integral part of rejuvenation, regeneration, and healing. To deprive yourself of this will lead to physical and mental problems. Often we disregard the uncomfortable experience of sleep deprivation as a necessary part of life thinking it does not have short term or long term effects on our body, career or life in general. Extensive research in sleep deprivation shows your are at risk for:

More stress, development of heart disease, diabetes and other chronic conditions, mood disorders, obesity, reduced immune function, increase accidents or making mistakes, loss of income, loss of job opportunities.

Benefits include: less stress, less inflammation, longer life expectancy, improves memory, creativity, ability to learn, decision making, performance, promotions and salary increase, improved weight control, less depression, less accidents (1 out of 5 car accidents), Better physical performance, less chances of injury, better sex life, better mood, and reduced immune function.

Here are some specific tools to make this happen:

- Go to bed by **10 pm** and have a set routine.
- Ensure that the temperature is right
- Ensure that light is not bothering you – or noise
- Remove cellphones from the room and any other reason to disrupt a full night's sleep
- Do not eat for several hours before sleeping
- Use sleep assisting devices – stay away from medications or supplements
- Create your body's natural ability to assume rest
- Meditate before going to sleep
- Plan the next day before – put to sleep your concerns for the next day by planning in advance

REMEMBER

Sleep is for restoration, rejuvenation, integration and for your health. - Bart Rademaker

Resources: Enough Sleep

http://www.drrademaker.com/enough-sleep/

- 28 -

Back To Nature: Vitamin G (green)

How much nature do you experience daily, weekly, monthly? Nature has a profound effect on all health and medical issues: would you invest in more of this vitamin G? Two to three days in nature enhances the immune system for a month!

There is the inescapable fact that for thousands of years people fully experienced nature. In fact for 99.9% of human evolutionary history, we have been in nature and it is only in the last 200 years that people have systematically reduced their experience of nature to the point that children today at a ratio of 10:1 prefer watching tv or playing computer games than saving the environment.

Whilst it appears that for many the experience of nature is rapidly dwindling, 35% reduction in the last 4 decades, it is becoming increasingly clear that nature is essential for our health and well being. Studies confirm that most diseased organ systems benefit from the effect of nature. This benefit is not only due to exercise itself, it is the actual experience of nature that makes the difference.

Hang out in the woods or take a regular shower of green and feel the comforting effects of nature. It is our natural habit - and to get the most out of it, find a park close by and fully experience it. By fully experiencing it, put away any of the distractions like phones or responsibilities. Find your presence in the nature and observe with your five senses. Walk or sit, write or ponder and absorb all the healing essence of the experience. Feel the ground and smell the different scents and observe natural movement. Discover more relaxation, more happiness, enhance immune function, better cognition, new creative impulses and solutions to old problems.

This is what vitamin G (green) will help you have more of:

- Feeling of connectedness
- Increased creativity
- Holistic living
- Sustainable living

Our successful growth, development and existence from birth onwards is intimately dependent on our relationship with our environment and most specifically on nature. Essentially, we came from nature and will go back to nature and how we treat nature is how our life will be. We can find better health, cognition, empathy and happiness by having the ritual to experience nature by going to it, or bringing it to our homes. We owe it to ourselves to do this and maintain a healthy perspective on a sustainable future with nature by doing so.

REMEMBER

It's natural to be in nature. -Bart Rademaker

Resource: Back To Nature: Vitamin G (green)

http://www.drrademaker.com/back-to-nature-vitamin-g-green/

- 29 -

Be Creative

What does creative mean to you? Are you creative? Would you like to be more creative?

In this rapidly changing world – we must be able to adapt easily in order to stay with the times. "adapt or perish" as some would say. Personal creativity is a great tool that enhances critical thinking, openness to new ideas and concepts. It can help with problem solving, boost self confidence and contribute to ongoing success. Creativity also promotes intrinsic motivation and personal reward with our own accomplishments. Experiencing creativity is like experiencing victory.

Creativity takes on many different definitions. In context of rituals and habits, it relates to your personal creative thought or manifested creations.

Find something that you would like to create – in writing, art, photography, ideas, or projects that allow you to expand your own mind, take new chances, try out new things, take risks and enjoy.

Make personal achievement be your new standard. All great artists practiced endlessly for many years before they received any recognition. This creativity is finding your *own* recognition and fulfillment with what you do create. It is not about a comparison but it is about some degree of dedication to practice and patience with the results and in the enjoyment of the actual process. Follow someone else's design or follow your own. Learn from the masters: model success.

Benefits from being creative:

- Expanded sense of time
- Brain expansion of neural networks and growth
- Sense of freedom
- Self awareness and expression
- Belief in self and self confidence
- Sense of purpose and accomplishment
- Stress relief, and a positive impact on health
- Redefine failure and iteration – learn from failure
- Commitment to mastery (work hard at mastery)
- Have fun, enjoyment, playful
- Enhances spontaneity which is beneficial in relationships

REMEMBER

Creativity is intelligence having fun -Albert Einstein

Resource: 29 Be Creative

http://www.drrademaker.com/be-creative/

An experience of creativity is an experience of joyous victory -Bart Rademaker

- 30 -

Retreat: Rejuvenate, Regenerate, and Replenish!

Top athletes are very familiar with these concepts: are you? Sustained activity without a break and without the opportunity to recover results in either weakening or complete breakdown with injury. What do you do to schedule personal recovery time or do you wait till your body is so weak, run down, it temporarily shuts down with an illness or injury?

The typical American lifestyle knows no breaks whilst European cultures require it and modern companies schedule it. Science has proven that sustained activity results in a decreased productivity whilst appropriate time off from works increases it.

Uninterrupted busy life is actually uncompromising because there is not enough time for the brain to create new neural networks that offer new possibilities. In other words, the brain does not get enough down time to properly process, evaluate and re evaluate what is currently going on and therefore can not offer newer choices. Additionally the physical body requires time to replace and reconstruct cells or tissues that are damaged through sustained activity as well as remove any unwanted toxins or cells that can further damage organs systems.

Scheduled time off during the day and during the week are critical for re balancing of the mind and body. If it is done with intention, it will be even more beneficial. A vacation away from the regular busy life is great to heighten personal experiences, connections and a chance to escape the daily stresses of life.

A retreat of several days to a week is indispensable to a balanced and healthy being as it can offer:

A time to slow down or stop and reflect on all things that are important or unimportant and discover new meaning or appreciation.

An opportunity to process, release and let go of unwanted burdens and to declutter, simplify and make room for new.

Develop new habits that nurtures your overall wellbeing and health including a means to detoxify and cleanse your body providing energy to revitalize and reconstruct.

Discover new things and new things about yourself and time to reflect and make new decision about your future.

Time for self, to think, to dream to create.

In summary, a retreat improves the quality of your life in all dimensions.

<u>REMEMBER</u>
To retreat – is to move away from any threats to personal well being and to create new opportunities or pathways for thriving
- Bart Rademaker

Resource: Retreat: Rejuvenate, Regenerate, and Replenish!
http://www.drrademaker.com/retreat-rejuvenate-regenerate-and-replenish/

- 31 -

Create Your Own Personal Retreat

Is your home environment a source of peace and tranquility? Can you escape the stresses of daily life on a regular basis? What if you created your own retreat at your own very home – on a limited budget – even with a household full of children?

Our minds need to shut down regularly – if only to process all the day to day information that we receive so that the mind can better function. In addition the body needs time to specifically recharge itself. If this is not enough to convince you – then notice any aches or pains or other types of discomfort in the body – these are all signals that the body needs more time to recover and regenerate.

Your home however small or large can be converted into your sanctuary. It only requires three things:
1. A clean and uncluttered space
2. A quiet environment that you confidently know will not be interrupted
3. Uplifting and inspiring elements to enhance your experience of wellness and healing.

To manage the first: clean and declutter the space or home with hired help. Create as much of cleanliness and freshness in the space without any clutter. Disposing all the clutter helps since this occupies your mind energetically – especially items that have any type of negativity association with them. Remove toxic chemicals – these are harmful to you and the environment. If you can Feng shui the space by either reviewing a book on feng shui and make it a fun project with that intention to create a better energy space for you. You can also hire a specialist in Feng shui.

Second, create quietness without any interruption during the period of retreat. Advise friends, family, coworkers or your clients that you will not be taking any calls. Turn off any distracting noises or technology including the computer.

Let your family know that you are not to be disturbed for any reason even though you may be in their presence. It is important for you to know that you will have this sacred time. Your mind needs the break. Your body needs the release from the stresses of modern world. Warn others of your plans and make sure they respect your needs.

Finally, surround yourself with elements that enhance your mood and experience. Get a massage in your own home, cater some specialized organic food, enhance the scent of the space with candles or a diffuser with essential oils, create real sounds of trickling water, or use any sound system for nature sounds or soft music. Lighting is important, dim it or bring in colors. Bring nature in the space in the form of plants or flowers.

Other items that can enhance your overall experience, have a juicer or nutribullet and create your own nurturing foods out of fresh fruits or vegetables. Infra red diffuser, tower garden, Water filtration system, earthing sheets and pad to recreate other nurturing habits.

As you prepare for your home retreat: have a clear intention and schedule of activities to support you. Turn off the TV, phone and computer. Don't do chores or attend to any other distraction during this sacred time. This is the time to reflect, daydream, celebrate, find stillness, meditate, be open and accepting, relax and enjoy, honor self, go for a walk in nature, be silent stop the urge to speak, listen to natural sounds or light music, notice things you did not notice before, focus on the important mindfulness of self, clarity of mind and purpose.

REMEMBER

The home should be the treasure chest of living. (Le Corbusier)

Resource: Create Your Own Personal Retreat

http://www.drrademaker.com/create-your-own-personal-retreat/

- 32 -

The Art Of Standing Up And Moving

Are you at risk for having the sitting disease? Have you actually heard about it? More than likely you are risk of having it if you have a traditional desk job.

Prolonged periods of sitting every day is a significant health risk equal to the effect of smoking on cardiovascular disease! Most people take the long hours of sitting for granted – an average of 7.7 hours total for the average American worker between driving, sitting at a desk and watching tv. In addition to the cardiovascular risk, all the body systems can be impacted by the long sedentary periods.

Scientific research shows that muscle activity during standing and movement actively stimulates processes that affect fat and sugar metabolism. When these are not triggered enough, inflammation and fat gain occurs. In addition, movement is important in the detoxification process of the body by stimulating the lymphatic system as well as helping the function of joints by the stimulation of joint fluid necessary for effective functioning and long term vitality.

Sitting disease, which is now officially recognized in the medical field, is considered a metabolic condition whereby the enzyme lipoprotein lipase becomes inactive in the blood vessels after 60-90 minutes of inactivity. This lipoprotein lipase enzyme is critical for metabolizing fats and sugars in the blood stream and regulates these levels in the blood. Lack of this enzyme causes weight gain, diabetes, reduction of HDL and increased risk for cardiovascular disease.

Other studies show that long periods of inactivity interrupted with a total of two and half hours of a work out during the week does not offset the cardiovascular risk.

It is important for your health to move every **60-90 minutes**!

Make it a ritual to move every **60 minutes**. Stand up, move around, create an excuse to take a break from work. This behavior actually will help your levels of concentration and productivity as well.

Make a commitment to activate your lipoprotein lipase and be healthier. Use an alarm on your watch, smart phone or other device or use an activity monitor that can either sync with your smartphone or computer.

Stand and jump on a rebounder for several minutes. If this is not available then stand and bounce on your knees whilst simultaneously shaking of your hands in front of you for several minutes. This combined activity will stimulate the body and lymphatic system.

Conduct short or even long meetings with a walk: outside or in the stairwell. You can go one step further and actually stand at work. There are stand up desk solutions as well as desks combined with a treadmill. Take this opportunity each 60 minutes to drink a sip of water to keep pace with your daily requirement.

Additionally, perform stretch exercises and even consider doing chair yoga!

REMEMBER
Life is motion -Bart Rademaker

Resource: The Art Of Standing Up And Moving
http://www.drrademaker.com/the-art-of-standing-up-and-moving/

- 33 -

Daily Tai Chi, Qi Gong
– Moving Meditation –

Implementing the ancient Chinese art of moving meditation delivers tremendous health benefits as well as increased mental clarity, balance and well being: could this easy technique be for you?

Just 15 minutes a day is your passport to better health and available to everyone independent of any physical or medical condition or level of fitness. Being that it is easy and safe to do by anyone and anywhere, imagine how easy and great it will be to benefit from the following:
Improved fitness, balance, improved agility & flexibility, increased aerobic capacity, increase energy and stamina, Improved mental focus, enhanced mental clarity, decreased stress and anxiety, enhanced quality of sleep, lower blood pressure, lower cholesterol levels, enhance the immune system, improved joint pain, improve congestive heart failure, sense of peace, tranquility, increase muscle strength/definition, improve overall well-being in older adults and reduced risk of falls in older adults.

Tai chi means great energy - a Chinese technique from the 12th century and it cultivates your life force through movement and is considered the martial art form of Qi Gong. It involves a series of movements performed in a slow, focused manner and accompanied by deep breathing.

Tai Chi is practiced as a graceful form of exercise, self-paced as a gentle physical exercise with stretching. Each posture flows into the next without pause, ensuring that your body is in constant motion and your focus is unwavering.

Tai chi has many different styles. The way to get started is to find a qualified teacher (sifu) in your area. You can also watch free online videos or purchase courses. Qigong, Tai chi are ancient practices that for thousands of years have benefitted those you performed it routinely. Make it your routine now.

Tai chi is an alternative to passive meditation promoting serenity through gentle, graceful flowing movements with tremendous health benefits.

REMEMBER
The doctor of the future will give no medicine, but will interest his patients in the care of the human frame -Thomas Alva Edison

Resource: Daily tai chi, qigong – moving meditation
http://www.drrademaker.com/daily-tai-chi-moving-meditation/

- 34 -

Earthing

Why do you wear shoes? When do you not wear them? How often do you go barefoot on natural ground? Do you notice feeling differently when you walk barefoot?

For millennia, humans were predominantly barefoot walkers. This provided a healthy balancing of the body (grounding) because of the conduction of the earth's electromagnetic field onto our bodies. This grounding – like modern appliances that require it for adequate functioning is actually what our bodies require for adequate functioning as well. The physiological processes in the body are largely governed by chemical and electrical processes combined with energy exchanges.

During normal metabolism, the body naturally accumulates positive charges that require balancing with the negative charges. Just like positively charged oxygen free radicals need to be balanced with negative electrons. If the body is not balanced, inflammation, irregular body rhythms, reduced immune function, clumping of red cells occurs as well as many other unhealthy conditions. The body requires a steady supply of negative electrons to function normally.

Because most humans protect their feet – the body is now insulated from the beneficial effects of the earth's energy and therefore sustain many of the aforementioned conditions due to a lack of negative electrons from the earth's surface.

Daily grounding by connecting with the earth's electromagnetism results in many health benefits including the following:

- Reduced inflammation
- Improved immune response
- Increased energy
- Improved sleep
- Less stress
- Reduction or elimination of chronic pain
- Thinner blood, improved blood pressure and flow due to less clumping of red cells
- Normalization of the body's biological rhythms
- Better skin conductivity
- Moderated heart rate variability
- Improved glucose regulation
- Less risk of obesity and diabetes
- Reduced cancer risk

REMEMBER
Go Ground, go barefoot
-Bart Rademaker

Resource: Earthing
http://www.drrademaker.com/earthing/

- 35 -

Bio Dancing, Rhythm Dancing & Trans Dancing

Do you dance? If yes, how often? If no, why not?

Our bodies are designed to move and to move a lot. Our brains respond naturally to rhythms and to sound. Motion "is" life and life happens in all sorts of rhythms/cycles (night/day, solar, lunar and internal biorhythms over hours or days). If we allow it, it is therefore natural for our bodies to respond to rhythms in sound or music. This is how we can dance, and dance can be both your medicine and your meditation. When did you last dance?

Dance has been around for millennia, for spiritual rituals, deep healing and just for the pure pleasure of being spontaneous and being witnessed in an unapologetic expression of ourselves. The brain responds positively during dance and even when observing dance.

Dance can be the gateway to the authentic expression of ourselves when we release any of the bonds that hold us back. It is also the path for personal discovery, but busy life competes with the our time to dance. Trance dancing is the perfect vehicle to release, heal and discover ourselves as presented by many great inspirational teachers Like Gabrielle Roth: "rhythm is the dance, 5rhythms".

Many modern interpretations of dance allow individuals to experience spontaneous self expression to music and to natural rhythms. The dance can be experienced fully, with energy, abandon, connecting with the music and flowing with the music.

Allow your body and even your voice to express the deep feelings that you have in response to the music, the environment, other people and your conscious and subconscious mind at work.

Dance is a ritual that you can repeat monthly, weekly or even daily! It enhances personal awareness and connection with self and others. It can bring up positive feelings that might otherwise be bottled up and simultaneously release any contained negative feelings. If one truly engages in the music, the rhythm, the environment and the people – it leads to more joy, happiness and health.

Leading to health happiness and connection.

REMEMBER
To The Spirit belongs the Dancer -Gabrielle Roth

Resource: Bio Dancing, Rhythm Dancing And Trans Dancing
http://www.drrademaker.com/bio-dancing-rhythm-dancing-and-trans-dancing/

- 36 -

Capture Your Dream

What dreams have you given up on? What was once a passionate desire or ambition that has taken a back seat in your life?

As part of our survival instinct – we may tend to view our world in more negative terms in preparation for any threats that may come our way. Additionally and not infrequently as we grow up and even as adults, we are told to be serious, to be realistic, to not play and that dreams are just foolish or a waste of time. Often times, we just do not allocate much time to the very things that truly fulfill us.

So we play smaller than we should and put our dreams away. Which dreams have you given up on that you would like to recapture? What would your life be like if you did not listen to the naysayers and you did follow your dreams? Could you start now?

Dream big! Be ok with any dream you may wish to have and start writing them down. Capture these ideas in a journal and take time once a week to do this. We all have moments of brilliance where the genius inside of us is very creative and delivers us new ideas that can excite us. Capture those and capture enough so then perhaps you can live out some of those dreams.

Just writing the dream is not enough. Write down what you will feel when you achieve your dreams, how you will benefit, how others will benefit, who will you meet, how you will contribute to others and why you must do it. Then decide if you have the skills to accomplish it and if not, how you can get the resources to achieve your dream and finally, decide if it's worth it.

Carve out the time and schedule it to turn your dreams into reality but first – dare to dream and find the time to do it.

In following your dreams, make sure that you discover if there is anything that stops you from moving forward and decide how to overcome what prevents you. Additionally, have a timeline and every week or every month check in to see how much progress you're making. Are you indeed on track to fulfill the dream? This feedback is important because it allows for any course adjustments along the way.

You owe it yourself to live the dream "now" and tomorrow as well.

REMEMBER

Capture your dream. Follow your dreams while you now can! Someday you might not be able to! -Bart Rademaker

Capture Your Dream

http://www.drrademaker.com/capture-your-dream/

- 37 -

Whatever You Do – Do It Well

How often do you think of this saying during the daytime: "anything worth doing – is worth doing well!" Do you ever know you could be doing something better than you know you are actually doing? Great examples are cleaning the house, office or making the bed. Do you do a good enough job or an outstanding one?

What we do in private gets rewarded in public. How we do anything is how we do everything! In life, average effort gets no results, good effort gets you average results, excellent work gives your good results and outstanding work give you all the victory and rewards you could ever hope to experience. Expect more from yourself than anyone else and give additional value in everything you do and you will be rewarded beyond your dreams.

Mastery requires effort and repeated effort. There is an expectation that success should come easily and quickly. Truth is, success usually requires long hours of repetitive work. Many will not do what is necessary and therefore live mediocre lives (in their terms). Often times people feel entitled to get things for nothing.

Having outstanding results and experiences requires having high (outstanding) standards. In general, it requires just the same effort or energy to do something well as it is to do it poorly. Ultimately – there aren't any more hours during the day to do it either way – except that outstanding results generally can give you more freedom to do what you want.

- Commit to doing well and over deliver
- Over deliver on taking care of your body
- Over deliver in your relationship
- Over deliver with your children
- Over deliver with your work
- Over deliver with your mission

Completing tasks actually delivers the real fulfillment we might be searching. By focusing singularly on the achievement of one thing at a time invariably leads to more accomplished. Studies shows that multitasking is not as great as people think it is and therefore not as fulfilling as completing tasks one task at a time.

Additionally being busy is not necessarily the same as achieving or accomplishing anything. Results makes progress, doing is not the same as progress. Mindfulness and gratitude during the task at hand is also fulfilling and provides energy to help you complete the task. Be outcome driven not activity driven. And do it with the intention of doing it well!

REMEMBER

How you do anything is how you do everything! Choose outstanding with anything, receive all the rewards with everything!

Resource: Whatever You Do – Do It Well

http://www.drrademaker.com/whatever-you-do-do-it-well/

- 38 -

Interrupt Negative Emotions

Do you ever experience a negative emotion that disempowered you or affected you in such a way that it did not serve you or cause you to do or say something you wish you had not?

Negative emotions do happen and they are not always logical but somehow they would make sense since they wouldn't otherwise show up. Anger, sadness, frustration, are just some examples of what you might actually feel, and a result of some unconscious belief or experience that causes you to respond in this way.

Willing yourself out of a feeling is just a means to mask the feeling and not resolve it. To experience divine happiness, you need to resolve what makes you unhappy. It is up to you to make the changes in how you respond to situations that cause a negative emotion.

The first step is to simply interrupt the pattern. Not explain, nor justify the emotion but simply accept and acknowledge that it is there and then just stop. Be curious about the experience and decide – what if it was "just ok that you have this feeling". What if you can "just be angry, not judge it, not punish yourself for it, and not react to it either". "Just be curious with it". Somehow, this emotion must make some sense. Welcome it into your human experience and understand that this is just a result of a pattern, an internal program to react in a certain way to any given situation. Patterns or programs can be interrupted. These patterns or programs are also called memes and someone else gave them to you or help you acquire them.

If you find this difficult – Eckhart Tolle describes a useful technique – imagine yourself being the "observer" of you experiencing the emotion as the result of an experience that induced it. Can you feel disconnected from the emotion at that moment as you are the observer and wonder what really is happening?

Once you have been able to simply acknowledge the experience, the pattern or program with curiosity as to what you notice in yourself or another, then sit with it and ask the question – "what do I really want?" and proceed from this point.

The ritual is to interrupt the pattern when you have the negative emotion. Pick one, several or all to interrupt as they show up. Plan on doing it automatically and commit to this. Write in a journal what the experience is and what you would like to change. Another way to interrupt the pattern is to completely shift your focus on something else. Whilst this is a strategy that can be effective immediately it may not necessarily help you make actual progress with the emotion, unless you ultimately can resolve it.

REMEMBER
Interrupt the negative, it's not taking you to where you really want to go!
-Bart Rademaker

Resource: Interrupt Negative Emotions
http://www.drrademaker.com/interrupt-negative-emotions/

- 39 -

Vocabulary Shift

Have you ever noticed that every word has a spell – that's why they call it spelling! What spells do you give yourself or give to others? How much do you really notice about what you are really saying, the words you use?

In communication technologies there are two conditions:

1. What we actually communicate is like the part of the iceberg above the water level – what's underneath is truly the rest we need to communicate.
2. Secondly, we communicate primarily using body language (55%) tone of voice (38%) and words (7%). Whilst words are only 7% - the words convey all the meaning (even if we don't voice them out loud).

What words do you use to express how you feel? And if a picture is worth a thousand words, then the right word can be worth all your feelings in that moment. The English language has over 500,000 words of which 3000 describe all the types of emotions that we have. Most people will only use a limited number of emotional descriptors and the negative ones typically outweigh the positive ones. In addition we use many more negative descriptions of ourselves than positive ones. A vocabulary shift is simply the ritual to replace disempowering words with neutral or empowering words.

The emotions we feel and the words we use that affect our emotions – then becomes our experience.

Change the words – change the experience!

What words do you use that you want to change? Make the list and try it for 30 days and notice how your life is different.
Examples of empowering descriptors

How you feel in this moment: Great, grateful, outstanding, and inspired.

<u>REMEMBER</u>

Every Word Has A spell, Notice What Spell Is On You! - Bart Rademaker

Resource: Vocabulary Shift
http://www.drrademaker.com/vocabulary-shift/

- 40 -

Forgiveness

Is it truly easy for you to forgive? Do forgive more than not? What does forgiveness mean to you?

For some people it is hard to forgive. There is an unconscious reason for this – it may even be conscious. One reason could be that you were threatened in some way and this cannot be forgiven. Maybe the threat is still ongoing. Another reason could be that someone is morally wrong in your eyes and you will not tolerate this. Forgiveness is actually not about someone else – it is about oneself only. Forgiveness is about letting go and regaining your own generative center and move towards a positive flow in life.

We all make mistakes that can harm others and ourselves. Somehow, all of our actions do make sense. We all do the best we can with the resources that we have. If you can understand this, then understand that we are all motivated by positive intent – even though the actions can have negative outcomes either for oneself or another.

With this in mind, forgive with intention rather than logic or dictum. The purpose of forgiveness is to regain your own power and not allow yourself to be negatively influenced by the ills and harm towards you by others. Forgiveness releases the resentment and or need for vengeance – emotions that are corrosive to self and disempowering. Forgiveness is not about condoning someone's behavior but rather no longer making it a part of your life. Forgiveness allows you to return to your flow and make better decisions for self.

Develop the ritual to let go of past ills performed by others and / or yourself. Forgive yourself for your own ills and make the effort to amend your own ills and then let go.

Future harms are likely and be curious as to why they do happen and as to why you are affected by them. Be curious as to how you find yourself in the particular situation (again). We all do the best we can with the resources that we have.

Forgiveness allows you to let go of the negativity you are holding onto to. This negativity is the extra baggage of your life making it difficult or impossible for you to claim your true potential. Holding onto the resentment causes you to focus on something that no longer serves you. Forgiveness opens up new space in your life to bring in positive things and enhance your life experience.

What ownership do you have in the resentment? What specifically in you is causing the resentment? Perhaps this is a warning and could be an example for you to make some changes in you. Additionally, ask yourself this key question, in one year, two years or ten years – how do you want to feel then and how would you want to have felt now?

Forgiveness is an opportunity to become "more" and an opportunity to heal. Consider this – We are all flawed in some way, we are all wounded in some way and all of this make sense. If we can bring all this into awareness and acceptance, then we can make a change towards all that supports our life experience in a more positive way. If Forgiveness helps us reach a higher vibration, why not forgive ahead of time?

REMEMBER
Forgive in advance, be free in your future -Bart Rademaker

Resource: Forgiveness
http://www.drrademaker.com/forgiveness/

- 41 -

Celebrate Your Faults
And Your Weaknesses

Have you ever celebrated any of your faults. Is this a strange question for you? If it is strange – notice why it is strange for you. The truth is – this is your opportunity to acknowledge something that you now can change!

What if you did not have a particular fault or weakness – how would your life be different? Do you have faults or weaknesses you wish you really did not have? Here is another truth – they can all be overcome in one way or another!

The first step is by recognizing and bringing into full consciousness a part of you that you prefer not to have. Change happens only when you are aware of where you are and where you want to go. It requires honesty and truth as well as a desire for being better.

Step 1: Simply acknowledge a weakness or fault you do not like.

Step 2: Be curious as to what this actually means and do so without any judgment or punishment to self. In fact, give yourself some praise that you are willing to see the truth. This requires courage, humility, as well as the ability to be vulnerable.

Step 3: Understand that there is a reason for this fault, weakness or emotion - a story behind it all. It does not need to be understood or justified, it just is! Accept this truth and know there is an opportunity to change!

Step 4: Change can happen when you have a direction – ask yourself: what do I want?

Step 5: Commit to making a change and explore/implement new resources till the change happens.

Finally: make a list of (3-5) emotions, weakness or faults on a 3-5 card you no longer wish to have. Place them where they are easily seen. On the opposite side of each, write what you want. Review the card regularly focusing mainly on what you want to become "more of". As you review the card keep on asking: what is really true and how can you have more of what I want. Add new references about the truth that you want.

REMEMBER

"I choose my truth of what I can be that serves me at the highest vibration for my life and I can let go of what no longer serves me."
-Bart Rademaker

Resource: Celebrate Your Faults And Your Weaknesses

http://www.drrademaker.com/celebrate-your-faults-and-your-weakness/

- 42 -

Reading The Label

Do you read the labels of the foods you purchase? Can you understand what the labels say? What if you simply read the label of what you are eating and realized that this simple activity could entirely change your wellbeing in your 40s, 50s, and later because you make better choices for yourself and your family.

It takes a long time before the accumulation of all the toxic ingredients in your body will affect you. Many disease states are clearly related to the food that you consume. Realizing how your body responds to bad ingredients now will change your life forever. Design your future health history now by making better food choices and avoid the disease states that others "choose" to suffer because they "choose not" to think ahead.

It is not easy to discard the foods you once enjoyed when you are not suffering now. Read the labels and make a commitment to understand what you are consuming. Every time you shop for food – take and extra 20 minutes and review the labels. Know what they mean.

Here are some basic facts to consider:

- Fat: Saturated, trans fat or partially hydrogenated: increases the bad LDL cholesterol and reduces the healthy HDL.
- Sodium: Excess sodium raises blood pressure and increases the risk of cardiovascular disease
- Fiber: Great for digestion.

Words to watch out for: Serving size, Calories, Fortified, Enriched, Added, Extra, plus, fruit drink. Made with wheat, rye, or multigrain's, Natural, Organically grown, pesticide-free, no artificial ingredients, Sugar-free fat-free, or MSG.

Remember the food industry spends millions of dollars to get you to eat their product through extensive research and marketing. The food business – like any business is in the business to make money – and why shouldn't they do that? It is therefore your responsibility to make smart food choices and know what you eat. If you change, the food industry will too. It already is.

You are what you eat. Most diseases states are a direct result of what you do eat and what you don't consume. This is the easiest way to take control of your health. Love your body! Give it the right food!

REMEMBER
You are what you eat!

Resource: Reading The Label
http://www.drrademaker.com/read-the-label/

- 43 -

Breathing

The air that we breathe – in and out keeps us alive! It energizes and revitalizes every cell of the body. To be without it for even minutes is not compatible with life – and we take this for granted: 25,000 breathes per day!

Improper breathing or insufficient oxygen leads to a dysfunction of body systems. Poor thinking, emotional liability, fatigue and ultimately disease. If breathing is such a natural part of us and contributes immensely to well being – then we must incorporate a breathing ritual daily to maintain higher levels of health and wellness.

Benefits of deep breathing:

- Increased oxygenation to the brain and its effects on the pineal gland (which regulates various biorhythms)
- Mental alertness, reduction of negative thoughts and depression
- Increased energy
- Relaxation, stress relief
- Massage of all internal organs
- Helps with digestion
- Alkalinizes the body

There are many breathing techniques – here are just several of them

1. Breathe in and out very quickly with short breathes for 10-15 seconds. This increases energy and alertness
2. Breathe in quick four breathes and then exhale 4 quick breathes: grounds and energizes the body
3. 2-4-1 breathe in for a multiple of 2, hold for a multiple of 4 and exhale for a multiple of 1

4. 4-7-8 breathe in for 4, hold for seven and breathe out for 8
5. Box breathing, breath in for a four count – hold for four and then exhale for four, repeat

As you breathe – there are three parts to deep breathing: abdomen, lower chest and then upper chest. If you can only focus on one – focus on expanding the abdomen.

Breathing is always a fundamental part of meditation techniques that have been used for millennia. The benefits are tremendous – practice this diligently throughout the day – especially during times of stress and feel the benefits.

REMEMBER

Breathing is to be inspired. -Bart Rademaker

Resource: Breathing

http://www.drrademaker.com/breathing/

- 44 -

Be Inspired

What truly inspires you that you have control over – in other words – what can you do now to get inspired without requiring anyone else to help you? What wakes you up?

Is it through your own creativity or is it through someone else?
Commit daily to finding that specific activity that will create more enlightenment or inspiration. What excites you – what naturally elevates your mood no matter what?

- Is it listening to a certain type of music?
- Is it reading a certain type of book: art, poetry, philosophy, religion?
- Is it art, photography, going to an art gallery?
- Learning about history or science ?
- Meditation?
- Trans Dancing?
- Working out?
- Incantations?

Inspiration is about recognizing what is possible for you in life – tap into that world of personal possibility that helps you become more. Say "YES" to life!

Commitment to this ritual will energize you – get you out of the funk.

Get excited about your future. Get excited about who you are and who you are becoming.

Focus on what you have accomplished!

Take inventory of your successes rather than focusing on what you have not accomplished or what is wrong in life.

Surround yourself with voices that inspire and empower rather than the "naysayers" who say it can't be done!

Find Inspiration in Nature.

What is inspiration but nothing more than a deep connection with the greatness within yourself and outside of yourself. It is the feeling that all is possible and great and that you a great. The more examples you have of what is great, and what is possible, promotes more personal inspiration – this is how your brain works – by making more neural connections and build on the activity of the network of inspiration. The more you do it, the easier it is to tap into it.

REMEMBER
Inspire: Breath the magic in you and around you -Bart Rademaker

Resource: Be inspired
http://www.drrademaker.com/be-inspired/

- 45 -

Laugh

When was the last time you had a really good laugh, a totally uncontrolled laugh? What was it like to feel that good after the laugh?

Laughter is such a delicious experience of life! Releases tension, creates optimism, defuses fears. It is so inherently healthy to our lives – it's a wonder we do not have more of it. Interestingly, children laugh approximately 400 times a day whilst adults only 15.

Benefits of laughter:

- Laughter relaxes the entire body and boosts the immune system.
- Laughter increases endorphins, decreases stress hormones, relieves physical tension thus promoting an overall sense of well being; relaxes muscles for short periods of time; even creates a temporary relief of pain.
- Laughter is also protective of the cardiovascular system and helps you feel good and optimistic and helps improve your perspective of a difficult situation.

Socially, laughter is beneficial in defusing conflicts, enhances relationships and team bonding. It helps to reduce anxiety and stress and brings people together. Laughter helps you to release inhibitions, defensiveness and to forget judgments. You can become more spontaneous and experience more joy in your life.
Try it sometime soon and notice how good it feels to have that hearty laugh. And in the very moment that you realize how great it feels to laugh – make that decision to laugh more often and every day and feel more alive everyday.

Since we don't laugh enough – create the ritual to find more laughter in life – more reasons to enjoy, be happy, relax and let loose.

Ways to do it:

- Funny shows: Candid camera, Marx brothers, Charlie Chaplin, Benny Hill, Monty python, Who's Line Is It Anyhow?
- Publications: New Yorker cartoons, Mad.
- Go to a comedy club. Seek out funny people. Share a good joke or a funny story.
- Check out your bookstore's humor section.
- Host a game night with friends. Play with a pet. Play with your children.
- Go to a "laughter yoga" class. Make time for fun activities (e.g. bowling, miniature golfing, karaoke).
- Do something silly.

Laughter can be so medicinal that Norman Cousins used it to treat his illness and wrote about it in his book: Anatomy Of An Illness: As Perceived By The Patient.

REMEMBER

Laugh a lot, laugh often, laugh now -Bart Rademaker

Resource: Laugh

http://www.drrademaker.com/laugh/

- 46 -

Listen To Music

Do you listen to music daily? Do you notice how different types of music affect you differently? How do you respond to your favorite music?

Music is everywhere and for many it is the elixir for the brain – creating state changes that induce health, peace, excitement, focus and many other beneficial states. Since this is true and scientifically proven, why not tap into this amazing resource consciously and induce the states we need when we need them?

Music, rhythm, chanting and singing dates back to ancient civilizations. The great philosophers, teachers, scientists and doctors including Pythagoras, the father of modern medicine and science realized the vital importance of music in our lives and the natural order of things and health.

Current science is constantly proving what these benefits are and to name a few: Stress reduction, Improves cognition, Decreases blood pressure, Improves immune function.

Music activates multiple areas of the brain faster than many other external stimulus. Practitioners of meditation take years to attain a certain depth of meditation where the right type of sound can induce it instantly or in a very short time – providing health benefits. Through the release of neurotransmitters like endorphins, dopamine, and serotonin, mood changes occur as well as an improvement in alertness, performance and memory retention. The types of neurotransmitters released and the effects they have depends on what brain waves are induced.

Certain types of music work better than others but in general the ones that you like are the ones that will support you well.

Music also triggers certain anchors that you have developed over time – whether positive or negative. (anchors are specific events or situations that are strongly connected with specific emotions or thoughts). Additionally science has proven how music or sound effects water molecules and the growth of plants.

Binaural beats induce specific brainwaves that affect you differently and can induce many different states ranging from sleep, relaxation, alertness and accelerated learning and memory retention. See resources on binaural beats.

Listen to something you like on a regular basis to induce either more alertness or relaxed state. Get in the habit of having music or sound easily available so that you can influence your state. Schedule downtime with specific music planned.

Go to Itunes and find new music to listen to. Find new types of music as it develops new parts of the brain

REMEMBER
Music is in the air and in our hearts – sing to its beat and be happier
- Bart Rademaker

Resource: Listen To Music
http://www.drrademaker.com/listen-to-music/

- 47 -

60-90 Minute Work Cycles

Studies show that our ability to be laser focused on the job or during learning rapidly diminishes after 60 to 90 minutes. There is the temptation to wrestle through the reduced concentration by all sorts of means – however, mostly ineffective.

Notice how you do become mentally and physically distracted? Is the seat uncomfortable, is the temperature uncomfortable, what other distractions are there?

Clearly the mind needs a break to process all the bits of information. This is your opportunity to maximize your potential and efficiency by stopping every 60 or 90 minutes for a quick 2-5 minute break. Stand up, move and drink water. Take some deep breathes and reorient yourself to the task at hand.

As you re-engage: allow yourself to commit to the specific project or task with specific enhanced intentions. For example if you are studying – choose to easily and effortlessly review the material and integrate well for effective recall later. If processing administrative or financial systems choose to easily and effortlessly process the material with complete accuracy and enjoy the process.

As you get up from your station, experience gratitude and accomplishment for the work that you have done and expect the same or better results during the next cycle. Your body physiology will also benefit from the interruption of your static sitting position to a dynamic walking movement by the activation of many beneficial processes to support your health.

REMEMBER

Get up and move, live a more productive and longer life
-Bart Rademaker

Resource: 60-90 Minute Work Cycles

http://www.drrademaker.com/60-90-work-cycles/

- 48 -

Take A Break From Social Media

How much time are you on social media per day? Do you feel that you are on it more than you want to? Do you feel you are missing out if you are not on social media? Do you dislike social media? Do you avoid social media? Do you use social media to advance yourself personally or professionally?

Whatever your answer is, social media is a powerful phenomenon and has completely changed how we connect and interact with the world today: good, bad and ugly! Social media is here to stay and it is not something you really want to ignore either for personal or professional reasons. However, if you are not careful, social media can become an escape – an escape from anything that might be more beneficial or supportive to you.

When facebook, tweeting, other social media channels do not truly contribute to real personal or professional progress, they compete with the brain's resources that are actually wanting to deal with important things. Social media can be very addictive because of the strong immediate emotional impact it can have and thus may compete with the activities that do not provide an immediate emotional benefit but rather do have longterm ones that are better. In this way, short term benefits and immediate gratification of social media may compete with fulfilling your long term purpose in life.

Ask yourself – what is the real cost with the time that you spend on social media? What have you lost by being on social media? What is the real benefit from spending this time? Do you ever feel uneasy when on Facebook – if so why is that? Ask the question: what am I avoiding when I get on Facebook?

Use social media with intention – daily. Set up your goals and outcomes as well as set times to use it. Get clear: what you really want to use social media for and in what way can it serve you at the highest level? If you set a limited time for social media – what activities on social media must be filtered out? What are your personal rules in engaging on social media and can you commit to them? Can you rate the value of different activities as to how it keeps you on target with your purpose or is it just a distraction?

Clearly social media has tremendous benefits and has created more connections and interactions the ever before – so take advantage of this. Organize the day where you are not constantly in need to check in with fb. If you schedule your social media time and focus on the important things the rest of the day – you will be much more productive. Recognize when it does not serve you or it takes you away from developing the relationships you can have in real time with others.

Again – what is the true purpose that benefits you the most with social media? For many it is a distraction from truly becoming effective in life. For others it is a powerful tool to become more effective in life. What is it for you?

REMEMBER
I Am Calm -Just Taking A Short Break From Social Media!

Resource: Take A Break From Social Media
http://www.drrademaker.com/take-a-break-from-social-media/

- 49 -

Model Success

What does success look like to you? Do you know anyone who has the success that you desire?

To be successful, you need to know how to become the success you desire and then implement the specific steps or actions that will create the success. Find that person who has proven this process and simply model their procedure. If you model this process well, it is likely you will achieve a similar success. If you fail, it is likely that either you did not properly emulate all the steps or actions or the environment changed and a new set of procedures is now necessary.

There is more to success than following a set of action steps. If something worked in the past, it does not mean it will work in the future. Likewise if it did not work in the past – it may now work in the future. Like any software, a set of programs can deliver a certain consistent result. Modeling is no different – it's the application of a series of steps in the right order to achieve the same outcome each time. Decide what success you want to model and then follow their formula: believe, think and act like they do. Modeling is really that simple but not nearly so easily achieved. Any missing element or in the wrong order, then the outcome can be very different.

The following considerations are essential to successful modeling.

- What do I want? (**clarity**)
- Am I committed to get the results, specifically, results and rewards versus price (what must I give up and is it worth the price); what will it cost me if I don't achieve this? (**drive**)
- Who has the results I want (finance, physique, relationships, etc)? (**define**)

- What do they believe about themselves and about their success? What do I believe about myself? Am I aligned? (**truth**)
- What do they visualize or what is their personal motivation to succeed? (**why, purpose**)
- What do they think or say to themselves to get the success they want? (**incantations**)
- What are their action steps? (**behavior**)
- What rituals or habits do they use consistently? (**discipline**)
- What decisions must I make? (**decisiveness**)
- What has worked for me in the past? (**history**)
- What are the quality questions that they ask? (**curiosity**)
- What prevents me; what do they do that I can't I do? (**blocks**)

Summarized: clarity, drive, define, truth, why – purpose, incantations, behavior, discipline, decisiveness, history, curiosity, blocks.

Finally the most important part of modeling is feedback: Am I getting the results I desire and if not, what must be done differently? What part do I not know, am I missing or doing incorrectly? What will give me the results I desire? If it's Richard Branson, Einstein, Disney you want to model think, believe, and act like them!

REMEMBER
Success Leave Clues. -Tony Robbins.

Resource: Model Success
http://www.drrademaker.com/model-success/

- 50 -

Who Am I ?

Can you authentically answer the question with clarity: who am I? It is by no mistake that you are exactly where you find yourself – whether this gives you pleasure or not, hope or fear, gratitude or despair. There is an intelligence in this universe and you are part of it. By tapping into that intelligence – you will become more of who you truly are. So, who are you really?

At the entryway of many sacred monuments is the inscription – "Know Thyself". In our modern era of personal growth and discovery – Tony Robbins reminds us of this. He states: The strongest force in Human Behavioral Psychology is to remain consistent with how we define ourselves.

You are the summation of everything that defines you, by you! Change your identity – change your life. You don't like where you find yourself – change you!

Before you can really change – you must know who you really are. Not an easy task by any standard if you don't know what to do. Google who am I – and not many relevant responses show up.

You are you – the summation of all your thoughts, beliefs, emotions, and experiences.

Answer the questions:

- What do you believe about yourself?
- What do you believe about people?
- What do you believe about life?
- Why do you do what you do and what do you do?
- Which emotion predominates in our life?
- What is your job, career, mission or purpose in life?

In answering any of the questions, the secret is to be as truthful and complete as possible. To answer the career question with a simple job title like doctor, engineer or teacher is to not fully embrace the identity of who you really are. Include the descriptions of qualities that you believe also describe you. Adjectives like responsible, caring, fun, inspiring and dynamic leader.

Instead of just being a parent, could you be the teacher and inspiration and the guide providing your children with all the love and resources so that they can grow to be great parents themselves in the future?

Can you be a healer and the cure to pain and suffering and be the lifesaver for all those afflicted with the misfortune of being sick?

Write out a list of any attribute you believe you have or others believe you have or any you wish to have more of. Keep this list visible and refer to it daily. Own all that is or can be great about you and be that person you want to be.

REMEMBER
Be The Change You Want To See In The World. -Ghandi.

Resource: Who am I ?
http://www.drrademaker.com/who-am-1/

- 51 -

Happy Inventory

Are you happy with the range of emotions you experience daily? What would it be like if you mastered your emotions entirely throughout the day?

We experience our lives through the filter of our emotion: our experience becomes the meaning that we give it.

Which emotions do you experience on a consistent basis? Is it hope, stress, fear, optimism, happiness, bliss or something else? Our emotional state depends on what we focus on and what meaning we give it. Our focus is the result of what we allow to be filtered into our consciousness whether the source is internal or external. It is a choice what we focus on and the meaning we give it. However the programming that then determines our response may very well be unconscious! And so we may indeed lack the control we wish we had.

Our brains are wired for survival: to find the dangers outside of us. You are more likely to pick up a newspaper that warns you of some imminent danger looming over the horizon versus something that is not so urgent! It makes sense! Many of us habitually will pay more attention to what is wrong or missing out of our lives or be critical of ourselves and focus what we have not achieved. All this is a result of our programming – be it from our upbringing, culture or other influences.

Take inventory of all the negative emotions that show up in your day. Simply acknowledge that they show up and do this without any judgment. Somehow it makes sense that you feel this way. Your inventory must include a rating of intensity and frequency.

At the end of a day and then week review your results and make a decision: is this what you really want or can it be better? What will you commit to change?

Then here is your plan / intention you commit to: whenever the negative emotion shows up – be curious about it without any judgment. Appreciate what you are focusing on and the meaning you give it. Decide what you want to feel in that moment instead: perhaps the very opposite of it, perhaps a feeling of empowerment instead. What else could make the difference – What if you reviewed what you are grateful for in the moment. What could be a gift out of this and finally ask yourself, if you looked back in one year's time, how would you have preferred to feel instead?

REMEMBER
Choose To Be Happy Today!

Resource: Happy Inventory.
http://www.drrademaker.com/happy-inventory/

- 52 -

Future Pace It

How much have you thought of your future? Have you decided what that is going to look like or are you like so many that made a decision some time ago and now you are for the most part on automatic pilot? Every day is largely the same as the last one?

What would it be like if you could predict the future? Well you can! In fact this exercise is so powerful – you will actually predict your future past history. Your story told in 10 years about the coming next 10 years. Write your history of the future time as if you were telling it in 10 years, or 20 from now. By acknowledging a lifestyle viewed to the past makes it that it "already happened". Decide what you want to feel, want to experience, want to become. Answer the question once a month. Rewrite and rewire each time. Engaging into the future and evaluating how well you are on track.

Write down now what you want the next ten to twenty years to be like!

1. What would you want to know about all these years?
2. What were they like, what did they give you, who did you become?
3. What would your future person tell you today of all these years?
4. What would they tell you to focus on, what to remember, what to forget?
5. What to gain and what to let go?
6. What actions did you take to get the results you wanted?
7. How easy was it to accomplish all that?
8. What advice would you give?
9. What incantations or affirmations would you share?
10. Who did you influence?

<u>REMEMBER</u>

My future is now as I make it already happening
-Bart Rademaker

Resource: Future Pace It

http://www.drrademaker.com/future-pace-it/

Register This Book at:
52WeekSuccessPlanBook.com
For additional tips, resources, and videos

www.ingramcontent.com/pod-product-compliance
Lightning Source LLC
Chambersburg PA
CBHW052115090426
42741CB00009B/1813